W9-BKI-702

"Church leaders across many denominations will find this little book filled with practical ideas and good arguments that will help us cure Christians in our culture today of their allergy to church membership, pastoral authority, life accountability, and any limits to their personal freedom."

Tim Keller, Senior Pastor, Redeemer Presbyterian Church, New York City

"Brief, fresh, entertaining, and, above all, biblical. This is the explanation and defense of church membership you've been looking for."

Mark Dever, Senior Pastor, Capitol Hill Baptist Church, Washington, DC

"Practical. Convicting. Biblically faithful. Leeman reminds us that church membership is not a choice but a demand. The book is punchy and provocative, but at the same time it is permeated with the gospel of grace."

Thomas Schreiner, James Buchanan Harrison Professor of New Testament Interpretation, The Southern Baptist Theological Seminary

CHURCH MEMBERSHIP

9Marks: Building Healthy Churches

Edited by Mark Dever and Jonathan Leeman

Church Discipline: How the Church Protects the Name of Jesus, Jonathan Leeman

Sound Doctrine: How a Church Grows in the Love and Holiness of God, Bobby Jamieson

Church Elders: How to Shepherd God's People Like Jesus, Jeramie Rinne

Evangelism: How the Whole Church Speaks of Jesus, Mack Stiles

Expositional Preaching: How We Speak God's Word Today, David Helm

The Gospel: How the Church Portrays the Beauty of Christ, Ray Ortlund

Discipling: How to Help Others Follow Jesus, Mark Dever

BUILDING HEALTHY CHURCHES

CHURCH MEMBERSHIP

HOW
THE WORLD
KNOWS WHO
REPRESENTS
JESUS

JONATHAN LEEMAN

Foreword by Michael Horton

CROSSWAY®

WHEATON, ILLINOIS

Church Membership: How the World Knows Who Represents Jesus

Copyright © 2012 Jonathan Leeman

Published by Crossway
    1300 Crescent Street
    Wheaton, Illinois 60187

All rights reserved. No part of this publication may be reproduced, stored in a retrieval system, or transmitted in any form by any means, electronic, mechanical, photocopy, recording, or otherwise, without the prior permission of the publisher, except as provided for by USA copyright law. Crossway® is a registered trademark in the United States of America.

Cover design: Dual Identity inc.

Cover image(s): Illustration by Wayne Brezinka for brezinkadesign.com

First printing 2012

Printed in the United States of America

Unless otherwise indicated, Scripture quotations are taken from THE HOLY BIBLE, NEW INTERNATIONAL VERSION®, NIV® Copyright © 1973, 1978, 1984, 2011 by Biblica, Inc.™ Used by permission. All rights reserved worldwide.

Scripture quotations marked ESV are from the ESV® Bible (The Holy Bible, English Standard Version®), copyright © 2001 by Crossway, a publishing ministry of Good News Publishers. Used by permission. All rights reserved.

All emphases in Scripture quotations have been added by the author.

Trade hardcover ISBN: 978-1-4335-3237-5
PDF ISBN: 978-1-4335-3238-2
Mobipocket ISBN: 978-1-4335-3239-9
ePub ISBN: 978-1-4335-3240-5

Library of Congress Cataloging-in-Publication Data
Leeman, Jonathan, 1973-
    Church membership : how the world knows who repre-
sents Jesus / Jonathan Leeman ; foreword by Michael Horton.
        p. cm. — (9Marks)
    Includes bibliographical references and index.
    ISBN 978-1-4335-3237-5 (hc)
    1. Church membership. I. Title.
BV820.L44   2012
254'.5—dc23   2011045124

Crossway is a publishing ministry of Good News Publishers.

LB		29	28	27	26	25	24	23	22	21	20	19
24	23	22	21	20	19	18	17	16	15	14	13	12

To the members past and present of the
Capitol Hill Baptist Church

CONTENTS

SERIES PREFACE

The 9Marks series of books is premised on two basic ideas. First, the local church is far more important to the Christian life than many Christians today perhaps realize.

Second, local churches grow in life and vitality as they organize their lives around God's Word. God speaks. Churches should listen and follow. It's that simple. When a church listens and follows, it begins to look like the One it is following. It reflects his love and holiness. It displays his glory. A church will look like him as it listens to him.

So our basic message to churches is, don't look to the best business practices or the latest styles; look to God. Start by listening to God's Word again.

Out of this overall project comes the 9Marks series of books. Some target pastors. Some target church members. Hopefully all will combine careful biblical examination, theological reflection, cultural consideration, corporate application, and even a bit of individual exhortation. The best Christian books are always both theological and practical.

It's our prayer that God will use this volume and the others to help prepare his bride, the church, with radiance and splendor for the day of his coming.

FOREWORD

"It ain't those parts of the Bible that I can't understand that bother me," quipped Mark Twain, "it is the parts that I do understand." Sadly, Twain's remark might be said to indict many "Bible-believing" Christians, especially when it comes to biblical passages on the responsibilities of church members.

Just think of how Western culture affects all of us. Movie star John Wayne is often quoted as saying that he liked God until he got under a roof. Our singers croon, "Don't fence me in!" and "I did it my way!" And advertisers appeal explicitly to our narcissism: "Have it your way" and "You're in the driver's seat." With all this in the air, it's easy to want the benefits but not the responsibilities of belonging—to friendships, to marriages, to the workplace, and certainly to the church.

In part, the images of self-made individuals who pull themselves up by their own bootstraps have made us suspicious of institutions. Also, a regular succession of major public scandals, as well as a politics of resentment, impersonal and ineffective bureaucracy, and broken promises have shaken public confidence in leaders and institutions. Even people raised in churches have been let down, bruised, and abused by those who claimed to be Christ's shepherds.

But it's not just the culture outside the church that is to

blame. Much of evangelicalism has been forged in a piety that pits a personal relationship with Jesus against the visible church and its public ministry. In part, that's because evangelicals have wanted to avoid nominal commitment and formalism, which are good things to avoid. But in the process, we have tended—especially since the nineteenth century's Second Great Awakening—to criticize formal church offices and the ordinary means of grace in favor of charismatic leaders and extraordinary movements. "Quick and easy" has beaten "tried and tested." Rapid growth in numbers has counted more than slow growth in grace. Pragmatic results, not formal structures, have been viewed as keys to success. Along the way, many of us were raised with the evangelistic appeal, "I'm not asking you to join a church, but to accept Jesus as your personal Lord and Savior."

It's not surprising that, after successive movements of this kind, "getting saved" would have little to do with joining a church. And now there are even evangelical movements that drop church membership out of the picture entirely. They say to just show up . . . or not. One evangelical leader celebrates the dawn of the "Revolutionaries" who have somehow decided that *being the church* means *not joining a church*. Instead, these revolutionaries find their own spiritual resources on the Internet and in informal gatherings.

Then along comes Jonathan Leeman, not only reminding us of those many passages that we had pushed aside, but also having the audacity to say things like, "Christ does not call us to join a church, but to submit to a church." The church is not simply another voluntary society, like the Boy Scouts or the

Sierra Club. It's an embassy of Christ's kingdom. And kings do not offer suggestions, sell products, or provide resources that people can take or leave.

Leeman finds the ground between lawless individualism and legalistic authoritarianism, and Christians today need desperately to hear him out. He shows us that Christ's kingship is the only antidote to these extremes. Christ rules us in order to save us and saves us in order to rule us. Unlike the rulers of this age, Jesus doesn't ask us to shed our blood for his empire; he instead gave his own life for his realm. Then he was raised in glory as the beginning of the new creation, and now he is gathering coheirs into his kingdom who belong to each other because, together, they belong to him. The visible church is where you will find Christ's kingdom on earth, and to disregard the kingdom is to disregard its King.

Some readers need to be convinced of the biblical requirement—and blessing—of church membership. Others, already convinced, may wonder how the theory becomes practice on the ground in the church's life. What are the criteria of membership, and how do we negotiate legitimate "judgment calls" in a pastorally sensitive manner? What are the consequences, especially in cases where discipline is called for in doctrine or in life? What are the limits as well as the responsibilities of the officers in exercising their ministerial authority? These are big questions. And the author does not circle in the clouds, but lands on each of these practical issues raised by his scriptural arguments.

Regardless of whether you end up agreeing in the end, Leeman simply packs too much biblical wisdom into these brief pages for any Christian to easily dismiss. Not being a Baptist, I cannot go along with everything! However, I found myself shouting a hearty "Amen!" to the main arguments for church membership. More importantly, I found myself delighting once again in the marvelous provision of a Good Shepherd who has not only redeemed his sheep but also has figured out how to feed and lead them to the end.

Michael Horton
J. Gresham Machen Professor of
Systematic Theology and Apologetics
Westminster Seminary, California

INTRODUCTION

A Bigger Deal Than We Realize

You don't really want to read a book about church membership. I understand. Maybe someone handed this book to you. Maybe you wonder if it would be a useful resource for others. But honestly, the topic of church membership does not seem terribly interesting. You become a Christian, and you join a church. That's about it, right?

Sometimes church membership involves programmatic elements, such as classes and an interview. And the topic gets entangled with questions about the Lord's Supper and baptism. But beyond all this, is there much to discuss?

The first time someone told me that I should join the church I had been attending, I didn't feel too strongly one way or another. Maybe I was a little averse to the idea? I don't quite remember. Here's what I do remember: joining would allow me to move into the church-owned "men's house" for inexpensive rent in a desirable neighborhood. So I joined. No, I didn't mention this reason to the pastors who interviewed me. They didn't ask.

Still, my take on membership was easy come, easy go. It's not that important either way. What do you think: is church membership a big deal or not?

There are a few people who say that church membership is necessary, and a few who say that it's optional. But the majority of Christian folk, I assume, are somewhere in between. They have a vague sense that Christians should be involved with a local church. But they would also say it's not the most important thing in the world, so we shouldn't make too big a deal about it. If Christians spend several years hopping from church to church, or if they decide to attend one church indefinitely without joining, that's okay, too.

If you belong to this majority in the middle, I'm writing this book for you. I'm *not* writing it primarily for the person who is skeptical of church membership, though, if that's you, it might prove helpful, too. I'm aiming for the average church goer, church member, and church leader who have been going along with the crowd on this topic. You're not sure what the big deal is, but fine, you say, let's do membership.

It's you I am after. I want to answer a question that you are not asking but should be asking.

My primary purpose is to show you *what church membership is*, because it's not what you think it is. I'm not going to defend it, not directly anyhow. I'm going to present a vision for it. And here's my prediction: if you grab hold of how the Bible views church membership, it just might change the shape of your Christianity.

Membership in the Bible is an astounding reality. Aren't you just a little curious? You're not even wholly convinced it's there, are you?

1

WE'VE BEEN APPROACHING IT ALL WRONG

Imperium. I recently discovered this word. It's not a word you would pull out while chatting with friends over coffee. It sounds socially clumsy, like an overly intelligent thirteen-year-old. But I think it's a useful word.

It's what you get when you turn *imperial*, a word that you just might hear in coffee-time conversations, into a noun. Imperium means supreme power or absolute dominion, and it gets at the idea of where the buck stops in a society. Who is the authority to which all other authorities must answer? Who can make heads roll, literally speaking, without threat of reprisal, because it's in the job description? That's who has imperium.

Imperium is what Caesar had in Rome, as well as those kings in the medieval days who were always shouting, "Off with their heads!" In modern times, we would say that the state has imperium. There is no higher power than the state. The state is where the buck stops. The state alone has the power over life and death—the power of the sword.

So if you want to start a business or a school, you need

the state's permission. The same is true for soccer clubs, trade unions, or charity organizations. They exist by permission of the state, and the state regulates them. They don't regulate the state. They don't have imperium.

Okay, what about local churches? Do local churches exist by permission of the state? Now that brings us to an interesting topic. In fact, it's a topic that just might turn our present ideas about the local church and its membership upside down.

JESUS HAS IMPERIUM

Most people in Western societies lump churches into the same category as soccer clubs or charity organizations. Churches are one more kind of voluntary association, we say.

Alternatively, we regard churches as a service provider, like a mechanic who services your soul or a gas station that fills up your spiritual tank.

But are local churches clubs or service providers that exist by permission of the state, one more supplicant who depends on the mercy of the lord of the land?

It's true that you as an individual Christian should submit to the authority of the state. But remember that the state is God's "servant" and God's "agent" for bringing judgment (Rom. 13:4). Yes, the state possesses the "sword," but it does so only at God's behest.

It's also true that churches should abide by the laws of the land when it comes to regulations such as adhering to building codes (if it has a building) or paying any taxes on staff salaries (if it has a paid staff). In that sense, churches are like every other business or organization.

At the same time, there is one thing that should be utterly clear in a Christian's mind: the local church does not exist by permission of the state. It exists by the express authorization of Jesus. After all, Jesus has imperium, not the state.

To be a Christian is to know this: Jesus is where the buck ultimately stops. Jesus is the authority to which all other authorities must answer. Jesus will judge the nations and their governments. He is the one with final power over life and death. The state exists by Jesus's permission, not the other way around. States typically don't acknowledge this fact, of course. But churches know it's true (John 19:11; Rev. 1:5; 6:15–17).

All authority in heaven and on earth has been given to Jesus, and he gave his church the authority to march on the nations. His church will therefore advance like an army that cannot be stopped. The boundary lines of the nations won't stop it. The executive orders of presidents and prime ministers won't stop it. Not even the gates of hell itself will slow it down.

Jesus has imperium.

WE NEED TO CHANGE OUR THINKING

In case we are tempted to overestimate the authority of the state, the fact of Jesus's imperium should diminish it. The state is merely one of his agents with a specific mandate.

But the fact of Jesus's imperium should have the opposite effect on our view of the local church: it should raise it. The local church is also one of Jesus's agents, and he gave it an authority that you and I as individual Christians do not have. And this has radical implications for what the local church is and what it means to be a church member.

If you are a Christian living in a Western democracy, chances are that you need to change the way you think about your church and how you are connected to it. Most likely, you underestimate your church. You belittle it. You misshape it in a way that misshapes your Christianity.

We've all been thinking about the local church and its membership as if it's one thing, when really it's another. It's as if we've been looking at our immediate families (dad, mom, children) and calling them businesses. And now I'm coming along and saying, "They are not businesses; they are families! We need to start treating them differently."

Let me try in this chapter to put the whole vision out there with five big ideas, all building on the universe-sized reality of Jesus's imperium. Then I'll spend the rest of the book cleaning up the mess I make here: justifying, elaborating, and applying.

We'll start with what a local church is not. If you are a Christian, the local church is not a club. It is not a voluntary organization where membership is optional for you. It is not a friendly group of people who share an interest in religious things and so gather weekly to talk about the divine.

Nor is a church a service provider, where the customer has all authority. It's ironic that we refer to church "services" (yes, I do this, too). As I already said, it's as if we are telling people to pull into the church parking lot at 11:00 a.m. and get themselves serviced—"Tune-ups for your soul in sixty minutes!"

Maybe we acquired this understanding of the local church from the Protestant emphasis on the location of preaching and the ordinances. Maybe we've been duped by Western democratic society into viewing churches as voluntary associations. Maybe it's a century's worth of practice at being consumers. I'm not sure. But here are some of the symptoms of our wrong thinking:

- Christians can think it's fine to attend a church indefinitely without joining;
- Christians think of getting baptized apart from joining;
- Christians take the Lord's Supper without joining;[1]
- Christians view the Lord's Supper as their own private, mystical experience for Christians and not as an activity for church members who are incorporated into body life together;
- Christians don't integrate their Monday-to-Saturday lives with the lives of other saints;
- Christians assume they can make a perpetual habit of being absent from the church's gathering a few Sundays a month or more;
- Christians make major life decisions (moving, accepting a promotion, choosing a spouse, etc.) without considering the effects of those decisions on the family of relationships in the church or without consulting the wisdom of the church's pastors and other members;
- Christians buy homes or rent apartments with scant regard for how factors such as distance and cost will affect their abilities to serve their church;
- Christians don't realize that they are partly responsible for

both the spiritual welfare and the physical livelihood of the other members of their church, even members they have not met. When one mourns, one mourns by himself. When one rejoices, one rejoices by herself.

The basic disease behind all of these symptoms, the disease which, I admit, courses through my own veins, is the assumption that we have the authority to conduct our Christian lives on our own. We include the church piece when and where we please.

That is to say, we treat the local church like a club to join—or not. And this assumption leaves us conducting our Christian lives somewhat aloof from the local church even when we *do* join one: "Sure, I'm a member, but why in the world would I ask the church to help me think through accepting that job in Albuquerque?"

Please understand, I'm not just pointing the finger. These are my cultural instincts, too. I confess that I want to do things my way. I want to avoid taking responsibility for others.

But this is not the biblical picture. We need to take off one set of glasses and put on another. Are you ready?

THE HIGHEST KINGDOM AUTHORITY ON EARTH

What is the local church? I'm going to say a number of things to answer that question, but let me start here: the local church is the authority on earth that Jesus has instituted to officially affirm and give shape to my Christian life and yours.

Just as Jesus instituted the state, so he instituted the local church. It is an institutional authority because Jesus *instituted* it with authority. Now, I'm doing my best to avoid getting into a conversation here about the relationship between church and state, but here is what you must understand if we're going to have a paradigm-shifting discussion about church membership:

> Just as the Bible establishes the government of your nation as your highest authority on earth when it comes to your citizenship in that nation, so the Bible establishes the local church as your highest authority on earth when it comes to your discipleship to Christ and your citizenship in Christ's present and promised nation.

So Jesus has instituted the state by giving it the power of the sword. Narrowly, this means the state can take your life (under the authority of God's Word). By implication, this means it has the enforcement mechanism necessary for establishing the basic structures of society, such as deciding who is publicly recognized as a citizen.

Similarly, Jesus has instituted the local church by giving it the "power of the keys." Narrowly, this means it can remove a person from church membership (under the authority of God's Word). By implication, this means it has the enforcement mechanism necessary for establishing the basic structures of the kingdom life, such as deciding who is publicly recognized as a citizen.

LOOKING FOR THE RIGHT THINGS

So instead of starting with the idea of a church as a voluntary association, we need to start with the idea of it as the people of a kingdom or nation. Do you see what I mean by a category switch, like moving from a business to a family?

When people ask, "Where is *membership* in the Bible?" the problem is they're looking for something like a club to join, because the word *membership* is a club word. Clubs and political parties and labor unions have memberships. But you don't often use the word *membership* in relation to governments and the citizens of nations. You don't say, "So how's the membership of the British nation doing? Aren't you guys running, like, sixty million members these days?"

Clubs begin with a point of common interest. Service providers begin with a common need or desire. Churches have all this, but they have something more: a king who requires the obedience of his people. The church begins with this fact: Jesus is Savior and Lord. He has died on the cross for the sins of everyone who would believe and follow him.

This means the Bible doesn't talk about church membership quite as you might want it to. It talks instead about how God's people *gather together under his supreme rule*. It's interested in the citizens of a kingdom, not club members. Beyond this, the Bible talks about a church's unity with a number of other metaphors (family, vine, etc.). This brings us to the second big idea:

> When you open your Bible, stop looking for signs of a club with its voluntary members. Look instead for a Lord and his bound-together people. Look also for other forms of unity (brothers and sisters in a family, branches on a vine, etc.).

Is church membership in the Bible? If you're looking for

the right thing, it's everywhere. I'll try to show you in chapters 2, 3, and 4.

NOT A CLUB, BUT AN EMBASSY

Now, there's more to the church than its institutional authority over you and me. We need the idea of a church as a family, and flock, and temple, and so forth. But all of these other realities have to be set inside the authority structure of the local church, which is why I'm starting there. A church's authority *gives shape* to the family aspects of church life, the body aspects of church life, and so on.

So I'm going to use a number of biblical metaphors for describing what life inside the local church looks like. But I want to start with one that we can then build on, one that replaces the "club" or "service provider" idea: it's the metaphor of an outpost or an embassy.

Where am I getting the idea of an embassy? I'm getting it from the biblical idea of Christ's kingdom. A church is not the kingdom; it's an outpost or embassy of that kingdom.

What is an embassy? It's an institution that represents one nation inside another nation. It declares its *home nation*'s interests to the *host nation*, and it protects the citizens of the home nation living in the host nation. For instance, I spent five months of college in Brussels, Belgium. During that time, my US passport expired. If I had tried to leave the country without renewing my passport, I would have gotten in trouble. I no longer had valid documentation affirming that I was a US citizen. One afternoon I went to the US Embassy in Brussels and had my passport renewed. The embassy didn't *make me*

27

a US citizen that afternoon, but it did officially *affirm* it. Even though I'm a US citizen, I don't have the authority to officially declare myself as one before the nations. Yet the embassy's affirmation gave me the ability to continue living in a foreign city protected by all the rights and benefits of my citizenship.

So an embassy represents one place in another place of the globe. But what if I told you there's another kind of embassy, one that represents a place *from the future*? That's what the local church is. It represents the whole group of people under Christ's lordship who will gather at the end of history.

A Christian's citizenship, Paul tells us, is in heaven. He even calls us "fellow citizens" with Israel, which is interesting when you consider what citizenship meant in Israel.

Unlike Israel, however, Christians' homeland is nowhere on planet Earth. We're strangers and aliens. Christians must look forward to their homeland. They wait for the day when the "kingdom of the world has become the kingdom of our Lord and of his Christ," when every knee will bow and every tongue will confess that "Jesus Christ is Lord" (Rev. 11:15 ESV; Phil. 2:11).

But hold on. There is a place on earth where the citizens of heaven can, at this moment, find official recognition and asylum: the local church. Churches represent Christ's rule now. They affirm and protect his citizens now. They proclaim his laws now. They bow before him as King now and call all peoples to do the same. Here then is a third big idea:

> A local church is a real-life embassy, set in the present, that represents Christ's future kingdom and his coming universal church.

The idea of church membership immediately follows from this picture of the local church. What is a church member? It's someone who walks through the embassy doors claiming to belong to the kingdom of Christ. "Hello, my name is Christian." The embassy official taps a few keys on his computer and then says, "Yep, I see your records here. Here's your passport." The individual can now enjoy many of the rights, benefits, and obligations of citizenship even though living in a foreign land. But not only that—and here's the crazy part—the individual becomes part of the embassy itself—one of the officials who affirms and oversees others. To be a church member is *to be* the church, at least a part of it.

A church member, therefore, is someone who is formally recognized as a Christian and a part of Christ's universal body. That's not to say that churches always get it right, but it's their job to identify and affirm who belongs to the kingdom and who does not. This is the fourth big idea:

> A church member is a person who has been officially and publicly recognized as a Christian before the nations, as well as someone who shares in the same authority of officially affirming and overseeing other Christians in his or her church.

Church membership is more than this. Again, we need to talk about the family-ness, and the body-ness, and the flock-ness of membership, and a host of other things, as we'll see in chapter 4. But we start here because it represents the kingdom authority that Christ has given not to us as individual Christians but to us as local church members. Jesus didn't leave us to govern ourselves and to declare ourselves his citizens. He left an institution in place that both affirms us as believers and then helps to give shape and direction to our Christian lives.

The embassy-like authority of the local church gives individuals who mouth the words, "I'm with Jesus," the opportunity to demonstrate that those words mean something. The local church guards the reputation of Christ by sorting out the true professors from the false. The local church enables the world to look upon the canvas of God's people and see an authentic painting of Christ's love and holiness, not a forgery. And the local church lays down a pathway with guardrails and resting stations for the long journey of the Christian life.

The kings and governors of the nations are not careless about whom they recognize as their citizens. Would the King of the universe care less?

SUBMITTING, NOT JOINING

If Jesus instituted the local church with authority over us, we don't just join one like we join clubs or voluntary associations; we submit to them as we do to governments. And this is the fifth big idea:

Christians don't join churches; they submit to them.

Both church and government, after all, represent the authority of Jesus, albeit in different ways. Even pastors and church leaders must submit to the church in this way. They, too, must have their citizenship affirmed from the church through the Lord's Supper.

Now don't misunderstand. From the non-Christian's standpoint, a local church is a voluntary association. No one has to join. From the standpoint of the Christian life, however, it's not. Once you choose Christ, you must choose his people, too. It's a package deal. Choose the Father and the Son and you have to choose the whole family—which you do *through* a local church.

Also, a church exercises its Christ-given authority very differently than the state does. "You know that the rulers of the Gentiles lord it over them," Jesus said, "and their high officials exercise authority over them" (Matt. 20:25). Christian authority, he says in the next phrase, works by giving our lives up for the sake of others as he did for us (vv. 26–28). Christian authority also works by the tender, effective, and heart-changing power of the Word and Spirit, not by the manipulative powers of persuasion and coercion.

Still, Jesus means for Christians to willingly give themselves—submit themselves—to a local church. What this does and does not look like we will consider in chapter 6.

WHY CHURCHES ARE A NATIONAL AND INTERNATIONAL THREAT

My sense is that many Christians don't understand what membership is all about and why it's a big deal. But that's because we've been approaching the subject all wrong.

I can, however, point to two groups who understand the subject's importance really well. First, think about all the governments who have persecuted churches and their members. These governments have been wrong to view churches as a threat to their institutional power—Jesus did not give churches the power of the sword. But such governments have been dead right to believe that church members won't give final allegiance to them. They give it to Jesus.

Listen to how the fourth-century Roman historian Eusebius described one early Christian named Sanctus, when Sanctus stood before his torturers in the year AD 177: "With such determination did he stand up to their onslaughts that he would not tell them his own name, race, and birthplace or whether he was slave or free. To every question he replied, in Latin, 'I am a Christian.' This he proclaimed over and over again, instead of name, birth place, nationality and everything else, and not another word did the heathen hear from him."[2]

The second group who understands this topic's importance is all the Christians like Sanctus who have lived under persecution, especially state-sponsored persecution. These brothers and sisters have put their lives at risk by being baptized into a church. Don't talk to them about "voluntary membership," as if the church is a bowling league. They know the price of their new allegiance. That's why I almost wonder if this book will make more sense to them than to Westerners like me. "Blessed are those who are persecuted because of righteousness, for theirs is the kingdom of heaven" (Matt. 5:10).

Picture, if you will, a globe with all the nations of the world mapped out on it. Now picture one little embassy of light. It's a gathering of Christians, gathered together in the name of their King, Jesus. Then the point of light divides itself into two, then four, then eight, and so it goes. A new nation is growing, a nation set inside the nations. This new nation leaves the boundary lines on the map where they are, but it cannot be contained by the map's lines. The line makers don't have the authority to stop these unworldly citizens. The points of light cross all boundaries, spreading everywhere like yeast through dough, or like stars appearing one by one as the night sky darkens.

These are the churches of Christ and their members. The world has never known anything like them.

2

MEMBERSHIP SIGHTINGS IN THE NEW TESTAMENT

If our goal is to understand what church membership is, it may be helpful to take a quick stroll together across the New Testament landscape just to make sure we're all looking at the same thing. It's like buying a piece of land. You want more than the real estate agent's description. You want to take a walk and look around.

To do this, what would you think of traveling back in time to the first decades of the church's existence, starting in the early AD 30s?

Assuming our time machine appears somewhere over the North Atlantic, we fly south over what the Romans called Britannia. Looking down, we see Stonehenge, already two thousand five hundred years old. Not much more is familiar to us. London will not appear for another decade, when Roman soldiers will plant it.

We cross a channel of water and then fly over the fields and woods of Gaul, a land captured by Julius Caesar in 51 BC. Today the area is named France. Crossing the snowy Alps we glide down over dusty brown Italian landscapes and eventually the magnificent city of Rome itself, where Tiberius Caesar reigns.

Turning eastward, we hurry over the Adriatic, then follow the coastline along the Mediterranean Sea through the territories of Macedonia, Thrace, Asia, Lycia, Cilicia, and round the corner to Syria, all territories conquered in the previous two centuries by insatiable Roman battalions. We don't proceed past the Euphrates River, beyond which the Parthian Empire lies and beyond that the nascent Kushan Empire. Instead, we turn southward into Palestine and the Roman province of Judea. Judea was conquered by General Pompey ninety years earlier in 63 BC. Now it's governed on Rome's behalf by the biblically infamous Pontius Pilate and the Jewish puppet king Herod Antipas.

Our time-traveling craft touches down in the city of Jerusalem, and we step out onto the sun-cracked Palestinian soil. We cast our eyes around at the brick-and-mud houses, a few mansions, and in the distance, the Temple Mount itself.

The purpose of our journey is simple: to catch a glimpse of the earliest churches and their members. Do local churches exist? Do they practice what we moderns call church membership?

THE CHURCH IN JERUSALEM

Looking around, we find ourselves surrounded by "Jews from every nation under heaven": Parthinians, Mesopotamians, Cappadocians, Asians, Egyptians, Libyans, Romans, Cretans, Arabs . . . the list goes on (Acts 2:5, 9–11). They are gathered for the annual Jewish feast of Pentecost, and the bustling colors and smells make us think of a flea market.

Yet the first thing to strike us is not a sight, but a sound, a "sound like the blowing of a violent wind" (Acts 2:2). Our feet get caught in the rush of a mob until we find ourselves standing in front of a group of men who, somehow, are preaching in the native languages of all these people. The crowd sucks in its breath.

One of the men, Peter, challenges the people directly. He hearkens back to the great King David, who called the lately crucified Jesus "my Lord." Then he concludes with this slap to the face: "God has made this Jesus, whom you crucified, both Lord and Messiah" (Acts 2:36).

We turn our eyes to the listeners and wait for them to stampede Peter. Surely they will pronounce him a traitor and drag him back to the authorities.

But no outburst comes. Somehow, the challenge works. The crowd is "cut to the heart" and asks Peter what to do (Acts 2:37). Without hesitating, Peter replies: "Repent and be baptized, every one of you, in the name of Jesus Christ for the forgiveness of your sins. And you will receive the gift of the Holy Spirit" (Acts 2:38).

It's a daring move, since Jesus's own execution was surrounded by charges of insurrection. But Peter isn't trying to hide that Jesus is a king, even putting the claim into David and God's mouths. What's more, he tells the people to identify themselves with Jesus through baptism. It seems he wants to establish a marked-off people—a publicly identifiable movement.

Remarkably, the people respond in droves: "Those who accepted his message were baptized, and about three thousand were added to their number that day" (Acts 2:41).

It looks as if we landed our time-traveling machine in just the right place. This is the start of it all. Asking around, we learn that, before our arrival, there was "a group numbering about a hundred and twenty" (Acts 1:15). Then on this amazing day three thousand more names are added: James, Andrew, Lydia, Alphaeus, Procorus, Jimmy, Scooter, Alice. . . . The church is counting heads and keeping records. They know who they are.

GROWTH AND PERSECUTION

As the days pass, we rent some office space in a tent, start compiling our own reports, and keep watching as this group settles into a new lifestyle. They devote themselves to the apostles' teaching. They share fellowship, the breaking of bread, and prayer. They call themselves "believers" and share everything in common, including their possessions and goods as people have need (Acts 2:44–45).

This group is on an entirely different wavelength than the rest of the city. It's as if they are from somewhere else. The whole flock of them meets "together in the temple courts," and then they break up into smaller groups "in their homes" (Acts 2:46). The group also keeps growing: "And the Lord added to their number daily those who were being saved" (Acts 2:47).

Now, weeks and months are passing. More and more claim to believe the message. Pretty quickly, the membership rolls of just men reach "to about five thousand" (Acts 4:4). We ask ourselves if this group is simply interested in padding its rolls. Maybe they're a little too concerned with numbers?

Just as quickly, the answer is obvious: not at all. Somehow, the leaders are aware of significant moral lapses and act to correct them (5:1–11). Somehow, the whole "church"—what they're calling themselves now—still meets "together in Solomon's Colonade" (Acts 5:11–12). Somehow, the whole church wants to have members' meetings to talk about better loving their widows (Acts 6:1–2).

There's no doubt about it: these people spend time together and care for one another. So remarkable is their life together that, surveying the population of Jerusalem, we discover they are "highly regarded by the people" (Acts 5:13).

Of course, not everyone likes them. Twice the apostles are hauled in to answer questions. Twice Peter says a similar thing: "We must obey God rather than men" (Acts 4:20; 5:29 ESV). This group knows the buck stops with Jesus and no one else. They "never stopped . . . teaching and proclaiming the good news that Jesus is the Messiah" (Acts 5:42).

Still, life gets pretty hot for the church. Persecution sets in as the local authorities are provoked. One leader named Stephen is stoned to death. It even looks as if the chief priests get ahold of a list of names and addresses because one of their more zealous henchmen, a Pharisee called Saul, begins "going from house to house" and dragging church members off to prison (Acts 8:3).

Strangely, Saul's work has an unintended effect. Multiple couriers start rushing into our office with the same piece of news: "Those who had been scattered preached the word wherever they went" (Acts 8:4). The persecution is scattering Christians away from Jerusalem into other cities and lands.

We soon hear about disciples showing up in Samaria, Damascus, Lydda, Joppa, and Caesarea (Acts 8:14; 9:10, 32, 42; 10:24). Everyone begins to realize that Jesus did not come simply as a king for the Jews (Acts 11:18).

About this same time a whisper campaign begins in the Jerusalem church saying that Saul himself has converted and begun to preach in synagogues that "Jesus is the Son of God" and "the Messiah" (Acts 9:20, 22). Many don't believe it until Saul himself shows up and preaches "boldly in the name of the Lord" (Acts 9:27–28).

Things are temporarily looking up. The church of Jerusalem, now scattered "throughout Judea, Galilee and Samaria" seems to be enjoying a "time of peace" (9:31).

CHURCHES IN SYRIA, ASIA MINOR, AND BEYOND

We decide that it's high time for a meeting among ourselves to begin sifting data. One of us suggests the possibility that God *purposely* sent all these international citizens to Jerusalem for Pentecost, and then *purposely* allowed persecution to come so that the converts would be scattered across international borders.

Sure enough, right into the middle of our meeting rushes one of our friends from the Jerusalem church. He's out of breath and has to bend over and lean on his knees for support, but looking up and smiling he says that "news of this reached the church in Jerusalem" and "a great number of people believed and turned to the Lord" across the Syrian border in the city of Antioch (Acts 11:19–22).

Fast forward one year. We pick up a copy of the Jerusalem church newsletter—"The Apostles' Screed"—and read that "a great number of people were brought to the Lord" in Antioch and that "for a whole year Barnabas and Saul met with the church and taught great numbers of people" (Acts 11:24, 26).

Clearly, this is not just a Judean phenomenon.

And these Syrian Christians are the real thing. A famine hits us in Judea, but the disciples in Syria send provisions south. Thanks to Antiochene Christian generosity, in fact, we find ourselves sitting in a church member's house one day enjoying spit-roasted Syrian lamb accompanied by fig and lentil salad, grilled flatbread and goat cheese wraps, and grape leaves stuffed with rice pudding. Christian love is definitely delicious. Again and again, these Christians prove that they care for one another, and that their care extends across national borders and to churches beyond their own.

Now decades are passing, and we watch the church planting momentum build. Saul, now called Paul, takes one journey where he plants churches in Cyprus and Asia Minor, including such cities as Derbe, Lystra, Iconoium, and Pisidian Antioch (Acts 13:4; 14:20–23). On a second journey, he plants churches farther west in the cities of Philippi, Thessalonica, Berea, Corinth, and Ephesus, to name a few (Acts 15:36–18:22). He then takes a third journey to strengthen many of these same churches (Acts 18:23–21:26).

Not only do verbal reports make their way back to us; copies of letters written by the apostles to different churches do as well—to the churches in Galatia, Thessalonica, Corinth, Rome, and elsewhere. Paul even writes under house arrest: "I am an ambassador in chains" (Eph. 6:20). He uses his entanglements with worldly authorities to the advantage of King Jesus.

In general, the response of the governing authorities is all over the map. Herod Antipas arrests and kills church members (Acts 12:1–2). The Roman proconsul of Cyprus believes their message and converts (Acts 13:12), as does one synagogue ruler (Acts 18:8). Governor Felix sees an opportunity for bribe money (Acts 24:26). Governor Festus calls Christians "insane" (Acts 26:24). King Agrippa is provoked (Acts 26:28). And another Roman proconsul, Gallio, basically says, "Whatever," and waves it all away like a pesky fly (see Acts 18:17).

It's as if the churches and their members are straddled somewhere on the edge of society—a part of it, but not a part of it, neither fish nor fowl. A copy of a letter from Peter shows up in the office one day saying exactly this. He calls Christians "exiles" (1 Pet.1:1).

A CLEAR AND CONSISTENT PICTURE

We read and reread the reports. We jot down notes. And we try to see if we can piece together what the local church and its membership are. As we do, ten indisputable themes emerge in all our documents:

1) The church's very existence unifies around the message of a Savior and Lord. As we heard in that first day in Jerusalem, the words "for the forgiveness of sins" and "Jesus is Lord" come up again and again in our notes. The apostles proclaim it (2 Cor. 4:5; cf. Acts 17:3; John 20:31). They call it the way of salvation and the good news (Rom. 10:9; 1 Cor. 15:1–5; Eph. 1:7; 1 Pet. 1:3–12). And the Holy Spirit gives people the tongue to say it (1 Cor. 12:3). These Christians respect and defer to worldly authority to a point, but their ultimate allegiance is to Jesus. They call themselves "ambassadors in chains" and risk everything, even death.

2) Christians are ordinarily united to individual but interconnected churches. In the beginning, every believer was attached or "added" to the Jerusalem church. Then there's a transition phase when isolated disciples are scattered, as when Philip explained the gospel to the Ethiopian eunuch. But all this is missions frontier stuff. Otherwise there are no examples of Christians separated from churches. Quickly churches were planted in Antioch, Iconium, Corinth, and so on. These churches continued to communicate, to identify with, and to serve one another in times of need, even across national borders.

3) Christians collectively identify themselves as *churches.* We can hear this in how they talk about themselves: "Saul began to destroy the church" (Acts 8:3). "News of this reached the church" (Acts 11:22). "Barnabas and Saul met with the church" (Acts 11:26). "Herod arrested some who belonged to the church" (Acts 12:1). "The church was earnestly praying" (Acts 12:5). "They gathered the church together" (Acts 14:27). "The church sent them on their way" (Acts 15:3). "They were welcomed by the church" (Acts 15:4). The Christians use the word *church* to identify themselves in their life together. The individuals belong to something larger and corporate.

4) Christians possess a special power and corporate identity when formally assembled. Paul writes of when the Corinthian church is "assembled . . . and the power of our Lord Jesus is present" (1 Cor. 5:4). Later in the letter he refers to when they "come together as a church" (1 Cor. 11:18), as if they are somehow more "a church" when together than apart. This gathered assembly, it seems, has the power to do things, to make decisions and pronouncements on behalf of Jesus.

5) The first step of the Christian life is baptism—always. It's a given with these folks. "Repent and be baptized" (Acts 2:38). "Those who accepted his message were baptized" (Acts 2:41). "But when they believed Philip as he preached good news about the kingdom of God and the name of Jesus Christ, they were baptized, both men and women" (Acts 8:12 ESV). "Scales fell from Saul's eyes. . . . He got up and was baptized" (Acts 9:18). "Then immediately he and all his household were baptized" (Acts 16:33). "And many of the Corinthians who heard Paul believed and were baptized" (Acts 18:8). "And now what are you waiting for? Get up, be baptized and wash your sins away, calling on his name" (Acts 22:16). It's hardly surprising that Paul, writing the church in Rome, simply assumes that all his readers had been baptized (Rom. 6:3). This public identity marker is just a given.

6) Christians are commanded to separate themselves from and not formally associate with the world. Paul does not forbid relationships with non-Christians (see 1 Cor. 5:9–10), but he does tell Christians not to do anything that might risk formally sharing their Christian identity with nonbelievers. He tells them not to be "yoked together with unbelievers" since light and darkness have no fellowship (2 Cor. 6:14). Just as God wanted a clear line between Israel and other nations, so God requires a clear, bright line between the church and the world: "Come out from them and be separate, says the Lord. Touch no unclean thing, and I will receive you" (2 Cor. 6:17). There's nothing blurry about that boundary.

7) *The life and authority of the local church shape and orient the lives of its members.* This was especially clear in our first weeks and months in Jerusalem. The Christian life began with the authoritative framework: individuals were baptized, added to the church, and then gathered to hear the apostles' teaching. From there, the believers oriented their lives around other members of the church: their meals, their praying, their schedules, their financial and property decisions, their provision for widows. Was this pattern unique to those first months? The Antioch church's generosity with the Jerusalem church suggests otherwise, as do other episodes we didn't mention, like Lydia's generosity with the traveling missionaries. Instead, what we witnessed in those first months gave us the detailed picture, which didn't need to be repeated again and again in the records over the following years. Also, the letters we received give us glimpses of the same communal life (for example: Rom. 12:4–16; 1 Cor. 5:11; Gal. 2:11–12; 1 Tim. 5:9–10; Heb. 10:34; 1 Pet. 4:8–11).

8) *Christian leaders are made responsible for specific sheep.* Peter tells elders, "Be shepherds of God's flock that is under your care" (1 Peter 5:2). Paul says the same to the elders in

Ephesus: "Keep watch over yourselves and all the flock of which the Holy Spirit has made you overseers" (Acts 20:28). The elders know whom they are responsible for.

9) Christians are responsible to submit to specific leaders. The author of Hebrews writes, "Obey your leaders and submit to them" (Heb. 13:17 ESV). Clearly, the believers must know who their leaders are. Paul writes, "The elders who direct the affairs of the church well are worthy of double honor" (1 Tim. 5:17). The Christians know whom to honor.

10) Christians exclude false professors from the fellowship. In one letter, Paul tells the church in Corinth to "expel the wicked person from among you" (1 Cor. 5:13). Obviously, you cannot *expel* someone from a church unless they *belong* to a church in the first place. Elsewhere, Paul says to warn a divisive person twice and then "have nothing to do with them" (Titus 3:10). And John talks about false teachers who "went out from us" because "they did not really belong to us" (1 John 2:19).

A CHURCH *IS* ITS MEMBERSHIP

Adding all this up, one thing is obvious to our Jerusalem research committee: to be a Christian is to belong to a church. No one gets saved and then wanders around by him or herself, thinking about whether to join a church. People repent and are then baptized into the fellowship of a church. Looking to Christ as Lord means being united to Christ's people. It's automatic, like being adopted means you'll quickly find yourself at a dinner table with brothers and sisters.

The idea of church membership runs through everything

we read and hear. No, none of our reports present a Sunday school teacher standing in front of a class asking the attendees to turn to section 2C of their handouts for a definition of "church membership." But everyone—insiders and outsiders—knows who is meant when Christians refer to "the church" doing *this* or *that*: "Barnabas and Saul met with the church" (Acts 11:26). "Herod arrested some who belonged to the church" (Acts 12:1). "They gathered the church together" (Acts 14:27). To be a church member is to be one of the individuals who constitute a church. Again, they know who they are.

In fact, you simply cannot talk about a local church without talking about its members. It's like trying to talk about a team, a family, a nation, or, yes, even a club without talking about its members. It's what each of these things *is*.

BACK TO THE FUTURE

It seems we got what we came for. Several decades have passed, but it's plain that local churches existed from the very beginning of Christianity, and those churches consist of nothing more or less than their members. So, yes, they practiced "church membership," even if no one ever mentioned membership classes or membership rolls.

Still, not all our questions are answered, the first one being, what *is* a local church? The last bit of news we received about Paul in Rome was that he was preaching "the kingdom of God" (Acts 28:31). Clearly, it's not a club. People don't confuse their clubs with a kingdom. They don't call themselves ambassadors in chains for a voluntary organization. And they certainly don't put their lives on the line for a service provider.

So what exactly is a local church? Furthermore, what is a church member?

We can climb back into our time-traveling machine and return to the present to answer these two questions. Don't worry, no more time traveling for us.

On the ride back, one of us pulls out a pocket Bible and opens it up to the book of Revelation. It's a letter from John to seven different churches in Asia Minor struggling against temptation and persecution. Toward the end is a description of the Beast, who sounds a lot like Caesar and his claims of divinity and imperium. How does John encourage these churches? He points to a picture of Christ seated on his throne, with heavenly beings laying their crowns before him. Caesar is an imposter. Christ's rule alone is absolute. This is exactly what the churches need to hear to survive as churches.

Jesus is Lord.

3

WHAT IS A CHURCH? WHAT IS A CHURCH MEMBER?

Instead of first-century Jerusalem, we turn to a sidewalk outside of an Italian bistro in Washington, DC. That should make for a nice change of scenery. My friend Coyle and I had just eaten lunch and were talking about church membership. Then Coyle asked me this tough question: "What's the difference between two Christians who belong to the same church and two Christians who belong to different churches?"

Maybe you can picture me standing there, several new red marinara stains on my shirt, staring at him blankly. I wasn't sure how to answer.

But it's a great question for getting to the heart of what a local church and its membership are. Think about it like this: Coyle belongs to my church. My good friend Mike, who is also a Christian, belongs to a church out on the edge of the city by the airport. The question is then, how does my relationship with Coyle differ from my relationship with Mike? Am I obligated to the two men differently?

You could say that all three of us belong to the body of Christ and the people of God and the universal church, as in "the Church" with a capital C. Furthermore, all three of us are called to love each other, to pray for each other, to encourage each other, to rebuke sin in each other, and even to care for each other financially as occasion requires.

So what's the difference? What should I have said to Coyle?

If there is *no* difference, then we'd have to say that the local church *does not exist*. It would be like saying there's no difference between my relationship with my wife and my relationship with other women. That would be true only if the marital covenant *did not exist*. But the marriage does exist, and so there's a big difference in the relationships. Likewise, the local church does exist, and so it seems as if there should be some difference in those relationships. But what is it?

Here's a hint: my church and I are capable of exercising formal church discipline over Coyle, but not over Mike. That is, Jesus has given me, as a member of the church, a formal judicial role to play in Coyle's Christian life that he has not given me to play in Mike's life. But understanding what this judicial role is requires us to ask what the local church and its members are. That's the goal of this chapter and the next. And these might be the two most important chapters in the book.

INSTITUTIONAL AND ORGANIC

There are at least two ways for us to answer the question of what a local church is: we can answer the question organically or institutionally. We can look at the flesh or the bones.

People these days love talking organically. Flesh is soft

and yielding and pretty. The thing is, flesh without bones isn't very pleasant to look at, either. So we really need both.

To understand the difference, think of the marriage analogy once more. If we were to talk about a marriage organically, we'd talk about all the wonderful things that a married couple gets to do: live together, make a home together, engage in marital intimacy, have children, share confidences, and so forth. These are the wonderful activities that we associate with the marriage relationship.

To talk about a marriage institutionally, however, is to talk about the stuff that our culture understands less and less, and is starting to leave behind:

- "We gather in the sight of God and in the face of this company to join this man and this woman."
- "If anyone can show just cause why they may not be lawfully joined. . . ."
- "With this ring, I thee wed."
- "I pronounce that they are husband and wife."

Behind all of these Western phrases is the idea of what the Bible calls a one-flesh union and we might call a marital covenant. This covenant is the skeleton. It's the rule structure that builds a platform for the relationship and separates a man's relationship with his wife from his relationship with all other women, and vice versa. It's the hard-surfaced goblet that holds the wine of marital activity in place. Lose the goblet, and you pretty quickly lose the wine (see Prov. 5:15–16).

The world today likes the activities, but not the institution, which is why more and more couples live together without getting married. They want the wine but not the wineglass. Sure enough, everything's getting messy.

Then again, many people choose the activity but not the institution because they have watched their parents or grandparents stay hitched and stay miserable. "Those are the rules" was the explanation. They didn't witness their fathers tenderly pursue their mothers, or their mothers cherish their fathers. They only saw eyes staring into space and mouths numbly exchanging information. They saw life, vibrant life, only during the screaming matches. How ironic and tragic. That's not what we want either.

Both rules and activities have been ordained by God: bones and flesh.

And so it is with a local church.

JESUS AND THE KINGDOM

Let's start with the institutional description—the bones, the wine goblet. And this is what people today most commonly miss or avoid. The union of relationships that turns an ordinary group of Christians—presto!—into a local church is not a "till death do you part" union. But it is *something*, as the possibility of church discipline makes evident.

In chapter 1, we called the local church an outpost or an embassy. To elaborate, here's my single-sentence institutional definition of a local church: *a local church is a group of Christians who regularly gather in Christ's name to officially affirm and oversee one another's membership in Jesus Christ and his kingdom through gospel preaching and gospel ordinances.*

Yes, this definition is a little clunky, but every word is packed with purpose.

Before unpacking it, I want you to see where I'm getting it. You might have noticed that in chapter 2's search for membership sightings on the pages of the New Testament, we left out Jesus and the Gospels. Why? In part, it's because Jesus talked about the kingdom far more than he talked about the church. The epistles, on the other hand, have the opposite emphasis. Get this:

- Jesus in the Gospels mentions "church" two times and "kingdom" forty-nine times just in the Gospel of Matthew.
- Paul's letters mention "church" forty-three times and "kingdom" fourteen times.

Jesus talked about the kingdom. Paul talked about the church.

What's going on? This might surprise you, but it is Jesus's emphasis on the kingdom that establishes the church as an institution. Paul wrote more in terms of the organic church, which we'll consider in the next chapter.

What does Jesus's kingdom have to do with the church?

ONCE UPON A TIME, THERE WAS A KINGDOM. . . .

To answer that, let's turn to a story. Once upon a time there was a kingdom called Israel. As in all kingdoms, Israel had a king and a land and a set of laws. But unlike most kingdoms, the citizens of Israel had an especially important job to do: *Israel was to represent God on earth.*

It's as if God sent out a press release to all the nations of the earth, explaining that Israel was his, and that the nations should watch them to see what he was like. Was God merciful or unmerciful, just or unjust? Watch this nation to find out, said the press release. He had given them an elaborate set of laws so that they would know precisely what to do.

Sadly, Israel failed abysmally at its job. They acted like insecure teenagers who cared too much about the opinions of their peers and imitated the nations instead of imitating God. Maybe they thought they were too cool for God's law. This made the nations think that God was nothing special, after all. In fact, he must be a lot like them.

Then one day along came a man named Jesus, who said at least four kingdom-toppling things.

1) God was firing Israel. They were losing their job of representing him (Matt. 3:9–12; 8:11–12).

2) Jesus was the one who would now represent the heavenly Father (Matt. 3:17; 11:27; John 14:9). He was, in fact, God and the perfect image of God (Col. 1:15).

3) God was establishing a kingdom, not as a place like Israel, but as his rule over a particular set of people. And this kingdom was for people who were repentant, poor in spirit, and humble like children (Matt. 4:17; 5:3; 18:3).

4) The citizens of his kingdom, whom he would purchase through his death on the cross, would join him in representing God on earth (Matt. 5:48; Rom. 8:29; 1 Cor. 15:49; 2 Cor. 3:18; Col. 3:9–10).

Yet a kingdom like this with no land and no geographic boundaries had a serious political dilemma: anyone could claim to be a citizen in this kingdom. And Jesus predicted that all sorts of imposters would (Matt. 7:21–23; also Matt. 24:5; 25:44–45).

This in turn produced a public relations nightmare: such imposters would bring the king's name into disrepute. Remember, this kingdom was supposed to be for those who are repentant, poor in spirit, and humble like children. It was to be a new kind of society. But if literally *anyone*—all by himself or herself—could just start claiming to be a citizen, there was going to be a mess. Forget about any "new society."

The citizens of the previous administration were marked off by the fact that they lived in a particular land. And even when they left the land, they had a number of distinctives such as circumcision, the Sabbath, and various dietary restrictions. But how would a landless, borderless kingdom like Jesus's mark off its citizens? Who would exercise border patrol when there are no borders?

INTERMISSION: THE WHITE HOUSE PRESS ROOM

Before proceeding with this story of Jesus's kingdom, let's take a brief intermission. Think about what's at stake in the larger conversation about church membership. We are talking about representing God himself on planet Earth. That was Israel's job, right? Walk onto almost any college campus today, and you'll hear the campus pronounce in unison, "No one can claim to represent God." But that's exactly what we're talking about.

Are you beginning to see how important this topic is? No? Let me try another illustration. Let's suppose we walked away from the Italian bistro and over to the White House and walked straight into the press room. I once knew somebody who knew somebody who took me into the press room. He took a picture of me standing at the press room podium looking very out of place.

You might know the podium I'm talking about. It's often in the news. The presidential seal is emblazoned on it. Behind it are a blue curtain and an American flag, along with a suspended oval medallion that reads "The White House." It is, perhaps, the most powerful podium in the world.

From that podium, wars have been announced. Markets have been moved. Whole economies have been marginalized. International treaties have been explained. Millions, even billions of lives have been impacted.

Now here's my question for you: have you spoken on behalf of the US president from that podium? Have you stared into the studio lights and the cameras of the White House press corps and officially represented the president's mind?

I assume the answer is no. The president must officially authorize you to represent his mind. Not even his closest friends or family members take the global stage and presume to do that. The stakes are too high for anyone to do otherwise.

Okay, here's another question: have you ever spoken on behalf of Jesus and his kingdom? Has anyone authorized you to represent this king's mind?

Representing Jesus is no inconsequential office either. In fact, Jesus, we saw in chapter 1, has more power and authority than the president. His words will never fail. His decisions will impact all eternity. Jesus has imperium, we said.

My guess is that many Christians have never stopped to

consider whether it's legitimate for them to claim to speak for Jesus. Ever since the fall, we human beings have felt entitled to do whatever we want, and we carry that sense of entitlement right into our Christianity.

In truth, human beings do not have the right to do *anything* apart from God's authorization. And the same is true for Jesus's kingdom: we can only legitimately act where he has given us permission to act. An individual human being cannot suddenly decide that he or she belongs to Jesus's kingdom and therefore has the right to stand in front of planet Earth and officially represent Jesus. You would not claim to do that for the president. Why would you claim to do it for the King of presidents?

Okay, the intermission is over. What's the takeaway? It's just as presumptuous to assume you have the authority to represent King Jesus, the divine Son, as it is to assume you have the authority to represent the president of the United States—more so, in fact. Someone has to authorize you.

THE STORY CONTINUES: THE KEYS OF THE KINGDOM

We return to our story about Jesus's landless, borderless kingdom. Who has the authority for publicly declaring who is a citizen and who is not? For starters, Peter and the apostles.

One day, Jesus warned the apostles not to trust the teaching of Israel's leaders (Matt. 16:1–12). Their term of office had expired, and they would be vacating the capitol building shortly, carrying the contents of their desks in boxes. Then he asked them who they thought he was. Peter, probably on behalf of all the apostles, answered, "You are the Messiah, the

Son of the living God" (v. 16). Jesus affirmed Peter's answer, saying that it had come from the "Father in heaven." Then he continued:

> And I tell you that you are Peter, and on this rock I will build my church, and the gates of Hades will not overcome it. I will give you the keys of the kingdom of heaven; whatever you bind on earth will be bound in heaven, and whatever you loose on earth will be loosed in heaven. (Matt. 16:18–19)

This is the first of two times Jesus uses the word *church*. Here he is talking about the universal church: the assembly of all Christians from all ages who will gather at the end of history. Jesus will build this end-time assembly.

How will he build it? He will build it "on this rock." What rock? Theologians have long debated whether the rock is Peter or Peter's confession. In fact, I think you have to say both. Theologian Edmund Clowney writes, "The confession cannot be separated from Peter, neither can Peter be separated from his confession."[1] Jesus will build his church not on words, and not on people, but on people who believe the right gospel words (like the Word himself who became flesh). Jesus will build the church on *confessors*.

Jesus then gave Peter and the apostles the keys of the kingdom, which gave Peter the authority to do what Jesus had just done with him: to act as God's official representative on earth for affirming true gospel confessions and confessors.

The interactions between heaven and earth in this passage are amazing to consider. Peter rightly confessed who Jesus was, and Jesus said that Peter's right answer came from the Father *in heaven*. Though Jesus was *on earth*, he spoke on behalf of *heaven*. Then, in the very next breath, he authorized Peter to do the same thing—to represent what's bound and loosed *in heaven* by binding and loosing *on earth*!

Bible scholars sometimes talk about "binding and loosing" as a judicial or rabbinic activity, which is helpful for understanding this phrase. For instance, a rabbi might decide whether some law applied to—bound—a particular person in a certain set of circumstances. Jesus essentially gave the apostles this kind of authority: the authority to stand in front of a confessor, to consider his or her confession, to consider his or her life, and to announce an official judgment on heaven's behalf. Is that the right confession? Is that a true confessor? In other words, *the apostles had heaven's authority for declaring who on earth is a kingdom citizen and therefore represents heaven.*

I'm not saying that Jesus established a "church membership program" in Matthew 16, but he indisputably established the church (which *is* its members), and he gave it the authority of the keys to continue building itself—effectively the authority to receive and dismiss members. The authority of the keys is the authority to assess a person's gospel words and deeds and to render a judgment.

Two chapters later, where Jesus uses the word *church* for the second and last time, we see those keys put into action:

> If your brother or sister sins, go and point out their fault, just between the two of you. If they listen to you, you have won them over. But if they will not listen, take one or two others

> along, so that "every matter may be established by the testimony of two or three witnesses." If they refuse to listen, tell it to the church; and if they refuse to listen even to the church, treat them as you would a pagan or a tax collector. Truly I tell you, whatever you bind on earth will be bound in heaven, and whatever you loose on earth will be loosed in heaven. Again, truly I tell you that if two of you on earth agree about anything they ask for, it will be done for them by my Father in heaven. For where two or three gather in my name, there am I with them. (Matt. 18:15–20)

The passage begins with the picture of a brother sinning, and his sin is out of step with his confession of faith. Jesus then recommends four rounds of confrontation. In round 1, the confrontation is kept private. If the sinner repents, his confession of faith regains its credibility and the confrontation stops. His life matches his confession. He is, once more, representing Jesus rightly.

In round two, the confrontation expands to include two or three witness, as in an Old Testament judicial setting. In round three, the whole church or assembly becomes involved. If the sinner still does not repent, round four ensues, which involves removing the individual from the covenant community—treating him like an outsider. Sometimes this is called *church discipline* or *excommunication*.

Jesus then invokes the keys of the kingdom again: whatever the church binds on earth will be bound in heaven, and whatever the church looses on earth will be loosed in heaven. And Jesus is not addressing the apostles or the universal church here. He's envisioning a local church. The local church, it appears, has been given the apostolic keys of the kingdom. As a result, *the local church has heaven's authority for declaring who on earth is a kingdom citizen and therefore represents heaven.*

Jesus has authorized the local church to stand in front of a confessor, to consider the confessor's confession, to consider his or her life, and to announce an official judgment on heaven's behalf. Is that the right confession? Is this a true confessor? It's just like Jesus did with Peter. And it will do these things with the ordinances that are established in Matthew 26 and Matthew 28—the Lord's Supper and baptism.

Matthew 18, which is filled with even more earth and heaven talk than Matthew 16, presents a crystal clear picture of this authority in the context of church discipline. But the ability to remove someone from membership presupposes an overarching authority to assess a person's gospel words and deeds and to render a judgment. This authority begins the moment a person shows up in the church building doors claiming, as Peter did, that Jesus is the Christ.

The state's representative authority, we said in chapter 1, is seen most clearly in its ability to end a person's life. Likewise, the church's representative authority in Christ's kingdom is seen most clearly in its ability to remove a person from citizenship in Christ's kingdom. In both cases, the full extent of institutional authority is indicated by the power to decisively end a person's membership, through death in one case and excommunication in the other.

Yet it's the same authority that is exercised when "two or three gather in [Jesus's] name" (Matt. 18:20) and baptize a person "in the name of the Father and of the Son and of the Holy Spirit" (Matt. 28:19), licensing the person as an official, card-carrying disciple. As such, *when it comes to a Christian's discipleship to Christ, the local church is the Christian's highest authority on earth.*

No, it's not an absolute authority, any more than the state is. But Christ does mean for Christians to submit to the oversight of local churches by virtue of their citizenship in his kingdom.

Will the local church exercise the keys perfectly? No. It will make mistakes just as every other authority established by Jesus makes mistakes. As such, the local church will be an imperfect representation of Christ's end-time gathering. But the fact that it makes mistakes, just as presidents and parents do, does not mean it's without an authoritative mandate.

Does all this mean that what a local church does on earth actually changes a person's status in heaven? No, the church's job is like an ambassador's or an embassy's. Remember what I said about visiting the US Embassy in Brussels when my passport expired. The embassy didn't make me a citizen; it formally affirmed it in a way I could not myself—so with a local church.

WHAT IS A LOCAL CHURCH?

Let's return to my single-sentence institutional definition of a local church.

A local church, I said, is a group of Christians who regularly gather in Christ's name to officially affirm and oversee one another's membership in Jesus Christ and his kingdom through gospel preaching and gospel ordinances. Notice the five parts of this definition:

- a group of Christians
- a regular gathering
- a congregation-wide exercise of affirmation and oversight
- the purpose of officially representing Christ and his rule on earth—they gather in his name
- the use of preaching and ordinances for these purposes

Just as a pastor's pronouncement transforms a man and a woman into a married couple, so the latter four bullet points transform an ordinary group of Christians spending time together at the park—presto!—into a local church.

The gathering is important for a number of reasons. One is that it's where we Christians "go public" to declare our highest allegiance. It's the outpost or embassy, giving a public face to our future nation. And it's where we bow before our king, only we call it worship. The Pharaohs of the world may oppose us, but God draws his people out of the nations to worship him. He will form his mighty congregation.

The gathering is also where our king enacts his rule through preaching, the ordinances, and discipline. The gospel sermon explains the "law" of our nation. It declares the name of our king and explains the sacrifice he made to become our king. It teaches us of his ways and confronts us in our disobedience. And it assures us of his imminent return.

Through baptism and the Lord's Supper, the church waves the flag and dons the army uniform of our nation. It makes us visible. To be baptized is to identify ourselves with the name of the Father, the Son, and the Holy Spirit, as well as to identify our union with Christ's death and resurrection (Matt. 28:19; Rom. 6:3–5). To receive the Lord's Supper is to proclaim his death and our membership in his body (1 Cor. 11:26–29; cf. Matt. 26:26–29). God wants his people to be known and marked off. He wants a line between the church and the world.

What is the local church? It's the institution that Jesus created and authorized to pronounce the gospel of the kingdom, to affirm gospel professors, to oversee their discipleship, and to expose impostors. As I said in chapter 1, we don't join churches as we join clubs. We submit to them as we submit to the government.

And that brings us to church membership.

WHAT IS CHURCH MEMBERSHIP?

What is church membership? It's a declaration of citizenship in Christ's kingdom. It's a passport. It's an announcement made in the press room of Christ's kingdom. It's the declaration that you are an official, licensed, card-carrying, bona fide Jesus representative.

To offer another clunky definition, we can say that *church membership is a formal relationship between a church and a Christian characterized by the church's affirmation and oversight of a Christian's discipleship and the Christian's submission to living out his or her discipleship in the care of the church.*

Notice again the several elements that are present:

- A church body formally *affirms* an individual's profession of faith and baptism as credible.
- It promises *to give oversight* to that individual's discipleship.
- The individual formally *submits* his or her discipleship to the service and authority of this body and its leaders.

The church body says to the individual, "We recognize your profession of faith, baptism, and discipleship to Christ as valid. Therefore, we publicly *affirm* and acknowledge you as belonging to Christ and the *oversight* of our fellowship." Principally, the individual says to the church body, "Insofar as I recognize you as a faithful, gospel-declaring church, I *submit* my presence and my discipleship to your love and oversight."

In some ways, all this is like the "I do" of a marriage ceremony, which is why some have referred to a local church covenant.

Church membership, in other words, is all about a church taking specific responsibility for you, and you for a church. Clearly, the elders or leaders of the church have a large and representative role to play here when it comes to the church's oversight. But we'll get to that topic a little later.

Notice then how this definition helps to explain the difference between my relationship with Coyle, who belongs to my church, and my relationship with Mike, who belongs to another church. Coyle and I receive the affirmation and oversight of one embassy, while Mike receives these things from another. It's as though two of us get our passports authorized at the US Embassy in Brussels, while the other gets it done at the US Embassy in Paris.

CHURCH MEMBERSHIP

It's true that a Christian must choose to join a church, but that does not make it a voluntary organization. We are, in fact, obligated to choose a local church just as we are obligated to choose Christ. Having chosen Christ, a Christian has no choice but to choose a church to join.

4

WHAT ARE A CHURCH AND ITS MEMBERS LIKE?

Do you know what a mixed metaphor is? It's using two different images that don't fit together in a single utterance.

You might remember Jiminy Cricket from *Pinocchio* exclaiming, "You buttered your bread. Now sleep in it!"[1] or have heard the phrase, "Take a flying hike." To this day I sometimes repeat the words of Biff, the thick-headed bully from the *Back to the Future* movies: "Let's make like a tree and get out of here."[2]

Then there's humorist Dave Barry's description of the 1929 Stock Market Crash: "The nation's seemingly prosperous economy was revealed to be merely a paper tiger with feet of clay living in a straw house of cards that had cried 'wolf' once too often."[3]

Yet it's not only the comedy writers who mix their metaphors. Poets do as well, though their mixtures are more subtle. T. S. Elliot opens one of his poems with a line about "forgetful snow,"[4] and William Butler Yeats writes about treading on dreams.[5] Strictly speaking, snow cannot be forgetful, and dreams cannot be tread upon. But the unexpected pairing of metaphors in both cases allows us to see true things that we may not ordinarily see with more literal language.

You might have noticed that the authors of the New Testament often mix their metaphors, and deliberately so like the poets. Think of Paul saying to the Ephesians, "I pray that the eyes of your heart may be enlightened" (Eph. 1:18). Hearts don't have eyes, but mixing them up helps us to see something deep and profound.

PHOTOS OF PARADING FRUIT BOWLS

When the New Testament authors start talking about the church and its members, they push this mixing of metaphors into hyperdrive, like hitting the turbo button on a racehorse. Paul talks about being baptized into a body, as if one could be immersed into a torso. Peter talks about Christians as "living stones, itself a mixed metaphor, and then he says that these "living stones are being built into a spiritual house to be a holy priesthood" (1 Pet. 2:5). If I had written a sentence like that in my high school English class, my teacher would have picked up his red pen and gone to town. I'm not sure what he would have done in town once he got there, but at least he would have had his red pen with him.

When you open up the Bible and read what God says about the church, you find yourself staring at one big mixed metaphor. We read that the church is like a body, a flock of sheep, branches of a vine, a bride, a temple, God's building, a people, exiles, a holy nation, a royal priesthood, salt of the earth, the Israel of God, the elect lady, and on and on. The images keep coming, one piled on top of the other. It's like flipping through a photo album of images. Or maybe watching a parade. Or maybe reaching into a fruit bowl. I guess it's like looking at a photo album filled with parading fruit bowls.

In the last chapter, we considered the institutional local church: the assembly of believers that Christ instituted for the specific purpose of exercising the keys of the kingdom and making disciples through preaching and the ordinances. That is what a local church *is*. It's a key-carrying body established by Jesus for the sake of everyone he has purchased with his blood.

But ending our description here would be like saying a marriage *is* the marital covenant while saying nothing about all the activities that the marital covenant makes uniquely and wonderfully possible, such as partnership building and physical intimacy. The institutional view needs to be complemented by an organic view, we said. The rules of an institution, mind you, don't only constrain, they commission. They empower. They build a platform for activity.

The keys of the kingdom, followed by Christ's Great Commission in Matthew 28, enable Christ's disciples to grab hold of the wonders of the new covenant and put them into practice on earth. And this is where all the biblical metaphors for the church come into play: body, bride, temple, family, and so forth. We live out our body-ness, our bride-ness, our temple-ness, and our family-ness *through* the accountability structures of the church's judicial activity of member affirmation, oversight, and discipline. The institutional language of kingdom and keys, you might say, acts like the bowl that holds all the fruit or the album that features the photos.

Sure enough, Jesus's kingdom is not metaphorical, at least not in the same way as these other metaphors for the church. Jesus's kingdom *really is a kingdom*. He really does rule his people. But the church is *not really* a human body, a bride in a dress, a temple made of bricks, a family of biologically related individuals, and so forth. Those are metaphors. That's why we began with the idea of Christ's kingdom—to help us describe what the church and its members *are*. But then we need to turn to the organic church, or what a church and its members *are like*. These members are like a body, like a bride being made ready, like a temple, like a family, like a royal priesthood, and so forth.

That's why it's not enough just to say that the church is an embassy of official citizens. When I walked into the US Embassy in Brussels, nobody referred to me as brother as they do at church. Why do they call me a brother at church? Because belonging to a church is belonging to a family of sorts.

The church is unlike anything on earth. It's simultaneously family-like, body-like, flock-like—you get the idea. That's a hard picture to draw, even for the best artists.

THE IMPORTANCE OF BIBLICAL METAPHORS FOR THE CHURCH

Let me make several more points about these metaphors and why they're so important to understanding church membership.

1. Each one has a job to do for describing something about our union in a church. Each metaphor teaches us something different about what a church and its members are like. To describe the church as a family is to speak about its *relational intimacy* and *shared identity*. To call it a body is to say that its members are *mutually dependent* but have *different roles*. To refer to it as the temple of the Spirit is to say that God *specially identifies himself and dwells with these people*. The language of vine and branch communicates the church's *dependence on Jesus and his Word* for its life. Do you see?

Think about it in terms of union. The union of a married couple serves a different purpose than the union of two bricks in a building because they are different kinds of unions. But what's our union within our churches supposed to be like? Like a marital union? A union of bricks? What? Well, we need to borrow words and ideas from all these different images to be able to characterize relationships within a local church. Isn't that amazing?

So when people ask me, "Is church membership even in the Bible?" I'm half tempted to reply, "No, it's not in the Bible, at least not in the way that you mean." The Bible has a much richer and more complex vision of how Christians should live out their unity in local churches. It's as though we've been looking for apples when really we should be looking for whole bowls of fruit.

There's nothing on earth like the local church.

2. We need all *these images for describing a church and its members*. If all these metaphors or images have a job to do, then we need all of them. You cannot just pick your favorite fruit from the fruit bowl and leave the rest—"I'll take the apples and leave the oranges, thank you." No, you have to grab the whole bowl.

In other words, you should think twice before deciding

71

which metaphor for the church is most important. Some Christians in church history have tried to say that the church is more the body of Christ or more the people of God. But that's like saying I'm more a husband than a father, or more a father than a husband. I admit, my wife or kids might prefer one or the other, but I'm irreducibly both. You need the categories "father" and "husband" and a number of others to describe who I really am.

Unhealthy churches, even denominations, are sometimes the result of church leaders who have picked their favorite metaphors out of the bowl and left the others—they become all intimacy (family) or all hierarchy (body).

3. Each of these metaphors gets put into practice locally. Every biblical metaphor for the church becomes embodied—puts on a body—in the local church. The family, the body, the temple, the people—all of these descriptions of Christ's church don't just float around in the air. They become concrete in particular places. They get put into practice locally.

But don't all Christians everywhere belong to the family of God? Indeed, they do, but God gives you the opportunity to act like a family with your local church; you treat them first and foremost as your sisters and brothers. Doesn't the body of Christ extend to Christians throughout the world? Of course it does, but you live as the body of Christ in your local church. One of you gets to be the mouth, one of you the elbow, and one of you the esophagus.

That means you need all of them to describe every living church you have ever encountered. Right there at First Baptist or Second Presbyterian or St. Mark's Lutheran or Grace

Community or The Journey you have the people of God. You have the temple of the Spirit. And you have the body of Christ. You don't have just an arm or an ankle of Christ's body.

Paul's description of the body of Christ in 1 Corinthians 12 provides a great illustration of this. Is Paul referring to the local body in Corinth or to the body of Christ universally when he talks about the body and its members in this passage? Consider the sentence: "Now you are the body of Christ and individually members of it" (1 Cor. 12:27 ESV). That sounds local. But earlier in the chapter he had included himself: "For in one Spirit *we* were all baptized into one body" (12:13 ESV). Paul wasn't in Corinth. So is he talking about the universal church?

The issue is not so difficult when we remember that the universal church is present in the local church. The local church is an outpost of the future universal church. That means Paul leans now in one direction, now in another. When he writes, "The parts of the body that seem to be weaker are indispensable" (1 Cor. 12:22 ESV), I would argue that he's leaning into an emphasis on the local body. Yet when he writes, "For in one Spirit we were all baptized into one body" (1 Cor. 12:13 ESV), I would argue that he's leaning into a universal emphasis. In short, 1 Corinthians 12 is a wonderful illustration of how a local church should begin to embody today what Christ's end-time gathering will look like.

To state this the other way around, your membership in a local body now presents a picture of your membership in his end-time body. You might be content for the whole idea of "church" to exist in your head. But Jesus wasn't so content.

He wanted his church and your membership in it to show up in real time. As such, you cannot fulfill your obligations to other Christians and to church leaders without the local church, at least not in the way Scripture calls you to fulfill them. And other Christians and church leaders cannot fulfill their obligations to you without the local church. You need *a* body of Christ to be *the* body of Christ. You need *a* family of God to be *the* family of God.

How do you fulfill Jesus's command to "love one another" (John 13:34)? How do you fulfill Paul's command to "carry each other's burdens" (Gal. 6:2)? How do you obey Peter's words, "Each of you should use whatever gift you have received to serve others" (1 Pet. 4:10)?

You obey all these commands through your (membership in the) local church.

Here's another way to think about what's at stake: How should we respond to the person who claims to be "righteous in Christ" but never pursues righteousness? We would say that he was self-deceived, and we would urge him to repent. Those who have been freely given Christ's righteousness in turn pursue righteousness (e.g. Rom. 6:2; also 1 John 3:7). By the same token, how should we respond to the person who claims to belong to the body of Christ universally but never actually joins a body of Christ on earth? We should say the person is self-deceived and should repent.

Christ's body, the Father's people, and the Spirit's temple will fully gather in glory. But amazingly you can find imperfect expressions, outposts, or embassies of that gathering right now in the local church.

There's nothing on earth like the local church—it comes from the end of time!

4. *The metaphors aren't really metaphors but shadows.* You can see this in Ephesians 5. Paul writes, "'Therefore a man shall leave his father and mother and hold fast to his wife, and the two shall become one flesh.' This mystery is profound, and I am saying that it refers to Christ and the church" (Eph. 5:31–32 ESV). Paul is talking about marriage, but then he unexpectedly changes the subject. He says marriage refers to Christ and the church. Marriage is a symbol or shadow of Christ and the church. We get it backward if we think that marriage is the reality and that Christ's love for the church is a symbol of marriage.

It's as if God, before he created the world, said to himself, "How can I weave into the fabric of creation a symbol or shadow of my Son's covenant love for the church? How can I proclaim this universally, so that everyone sees it and realizes that they are standing in the shadow of something very, very big?"

Answer: he created marriage. It's the shadowy outline that points to the *real* reality—Christ and the church.

The same is true, I believe, for all the biblical metaphors for the church. They are the shadows of something even greater. Think also of Paul's reference to the heavenly Father "from whom every family in heaven and on earth derives its name" (Eph. 3:15). God placed earthly fathers on earth so that all the world would have a shadowy outline of what our relationship with the heavenly Father is to be like.

Why do you think God has created brothers and sisters?

Again, so that everyone gets a dim sense of the true reality that begins now in the local church and awaits us completely in glory.

What about branches on the vine? It gives us a dim picture of our dependence on the Word of Christ. I trust that in glory our utter, complete, and total dependence on him will become even plainer. Even Old Testament metaphors for the church, like the temple, though pointing backward to the life of Israel, point forward to greater realities in the age to come.

THERE'S NOTHING LIKE IT

Are you beginning to understand why I keep saying there's nothing in the world like the local church and its members? The relationships that we share in the local church will ultimately prove more interconnected than a physical body, more safe than a father's embrace, more collegial than brotherly love, more resilient than a stone house, more holy than a priesthood, and on and on we could go.

This is what Jesus has prepared for us in glory, and this is what we begin to practice right now at First Baptist or Second Presbyterian or The Journey. We practice it with all those still-sinful and still-strange people who step on our toes, just as we step on theirs.

What are the local church and its members like? They are like a body, like a bride being made ready, like a temple, like a family, like a royal priesthood . . . but in every case *even more*!

BACK TO REALITY?

Having said all this, every church member on the planet knows that life in the local church doesn't always feel this way—so interconnected, so safe, so collegial, so resilient, so holy. In fact, it can feel the opposite.

One woman recently left my own church feeling disappointed and hurt by our church. She wrote to me in an e-mail, "Regardless of whether they are believers or not, the members of my family will go to lengths for me like no church family ever would. And so, honestly, I no longer buy that family and community picture the way I bought it before. The family I've been born into and the friends I've had for a lifetime will be the people I can truly count on."

These are the words of someone whose hopes have been dashed. She was taught the church was one thing, and she experienced something very different. More interconnected than a family? More safe than a father's embrace? More collegial than siblings? Really?! Not in her experience. Maybe not in yours.

What shall we say about realities like these? Here's what I said to her:

> For starters, I'm sorry. I'm sorry for our sin and the hurt we've caused. I trust the sin is real and the hurt is real.
>
> Next, please forgive us. We need you to forgive us, so that we can be reconciled in Christ, even if we don't belong to the same congregation.
>
> Finally, will you look to the gospel with me? I think of Peter, this rock on which the church is built, promising Jesus that he wouldn't deny him, and then denying him. Later,

Peter wouldn't eat with an entire class of church members, the Gentiles. Still, Jesus died for betrayers and hypocrites and jerks and racists like this Peter. And Peter is the one who, later, talked about the church as "living stones" and a "spiritual house." Really, Peter? Have you been so strong, resilient, and spiritual with your brothers and sisters in Christ?

Here's the good news: it's not the strength and love of people like Peter that we have to rely upon and trust. It's the strength and love of Christ. Through his work on the cross, we have been made *his* body, *his* family, *his* temple, *his* people, *his* flock, *his* joy and crown. He has made us what we are, not us. Now, he's perfecting us to become what we (strangely) already are.

So hang tight. Stick with us. Persevere in forgiveness and love. We'll get there—not because of us, but because of him.

Your *brother* in him,
Jonathan

Twelve Reasons Membership Matters

1. *It's biblical.* Jesus established the local church and all the apostles did their ministry through it. The Christian life in the New Testament is church life. Christians today should expect and desire the same.

2. *The church is its members.* To be a church in the New Testament is to be one of its members (read through Acts). And you want to be part of the church because that's who Jesus came to rescue and reconcile to himself.

3. *It's a prerequisite for the Lord's Supper.* The Lord's Supper is a meal for the gathered church, that is, for members (see 1 Cor. 11:20–33). And you want to take the Lord's Supper. It's the team flag that makes the church team visible to the nations.

4. *It's how you officially represent Jesus.* Membership is the church's affirmation that you are a citizen of Christ's kingdom and therefore a pasport-carrying Jesus representative before the nations. And you want your representation to be authorized. Closely related to this. . . .

5. *It's how you declare your highest allegiance.* Your membership on the team, which becomes visible when you wave the flag of the Lord's Supper,

is a public testimony that your highest allegiance belongs to Jesus. Trials and persecution may come, but your only words are, "I am a Christian."

6. *It's how you embody and experience biblical images.* It's within the accountability structures of the local church that Christians live and experience the interconnectivity of his body, the spiritual fullness of his temple, and the safety and intimacy and shared identity of his family.

7. *It's how you serve other Christians.* Membership helps you to know which Christians on planet Earth you are specifically responsible to love, serve, warn, and encourage. It enables you to fulfill your biblical responsibilities to Christ's body (for example, see Eph. 4:11–16, 25–32).

8. *It's how you follow Christian leaders.* Membership helps you to know which Christian leaders on planet Earth you are called to obey and follow. Again, it allows you to fulfill your biblical responsibility to them (see Heb. 13:7, 17).

9. *It helps Christian leaders lead.* Membership lets Christian leaders know which Christians on planet Earth they will "give an account" for (Acts 20:28; 1 Pet. 5:2).

10. *It enables church discipline.* It gives you the biblically prescribed place to participate in the work of church discipline responsibly, wisely, and lovingly (1 Cor. 5).

11. *It gives structure to your Christian life.* It places an individual Christian's claim to obey and follow Jesus into a real-life setting where authority is actually exercised over us (see John 14:15; 1 John 2:19; 4:20–21). *It's God's discipling program.*

12. *It builds a witness and invites the nations.* Membership puts the alternative rule of Christ on display for the watching universe (see Matt. 5:13; John 13:34–35; Eph. 3:10; 1 Pet. 2:9–12). The very boundaries, which are drawn around the membership of a church, yield a society of people that invites the nations to something better. *It's God's evangelism program.*

5

WHAT ARE THE "STANDARDS" OF MEMBERSHIP? (BECOMING A MEMBER)

Some people dismiss church membership because they think it means making people jump through hoops. Or they think it means erecting standards of behavior for the sake of entry. Both of these things sound like the opposite of God's grace, which is free.

It's not hard to see why people think this way. Typically, membership involves meeting a standard of some kind. You have to be rich enough for the country club, cool enough for the in crowd, smart enough for the debate team, fast enough for the football team, and caring enough for the charity society.

To be a member of something is, by definition, to *be something* that others are not. And this sounds dangerously exclusive, doesn't it? Might not the idea of church membership tempt Christians to moralism or Phariseeism? Christianity is not about standards. It's about free grace. How then can we erect standards?

Truth be told, it's easy to move in a moralistic direction with church membership. Earlier I said that a church member is a passport-carrying Jesus representative, and I'm going to stick by that. But consider how quickly our thinking can go wrong: Jesus is perfectly holy. Therefore, representing Jesus must mean being holy. And that must mean that the standard of church membership is holiness. Therefore, I am going to look down on anyone who is not holy like I am. Maybe I shouldn't even let them into my church. They don't homeschool their children like I do. Or pray with passion like I do. Or go on missions trips like I do. Or make frugal purchases like I do.

Do you see where this is going? It seems as if the whole idea of church membership just might create first-class citizens, second-class citizens, and noncitizens based on how people *perform*. And that's antigrace and antigospel. Is that what this book is advocating?

What exactly are the "standards" of church membership?

WHO GETS IN?

One of the privileges I have enjoyed while serving as an elder of churches is the opportunity to do membership interviews. You might say that it's like standing at the gate of the sheep pen and being careful about what kind of animals get in. You want the sheep and not the wolves.

Based on what a person says in that interview, I may recommend the individual to the other elders, who in turn may recommend the individual to the entire congregation. Since Jesus gives the power of the keys to the local church, we believe it's finally the church's decision to make, not the elders'.

Who gets in? Here's the super simple answer: Christians.

That is to say, the standard for church membership should be no higher or lower than the standard for being a Christian—with one exception, which I'll come to in a moment. You're looking to affirm the sheep.

Church membership begins when a local church affirms an individual Christian's profession of faith. As Jesus did with Peter, we ask the person who Jesus is. As Peter did with Jesus, the person responds by saying that Jesus is the Christ, the Son of the living God—and knows what these words mean. In other words, people need to understand and believe the gospel to join a church.

People cannot always explain the gospel well, but in one way or another they must be able to explain it. They must be able to say who they represent before we officially call them Jesus's representatives. I remember one interview I did with a women whose first language was not English. When I asked her what the gospel was, she looked at me quizzically and said, "The gospel?" as if she had never heard the word before. I followed up by saying, "The good news of Jesus Christ." This clarification flipped a mental switch for her, and she explained the gospel just fine. Our church began calling her a member. To do so is like sending a press release: "To the nations: You may now look to this woman to know what Jesus is like. She is an official Jesus representative."

Other times I have interviewed individuals who could not explain the gospel. I remember another woman telling me that being a Christian means "doing your best." I tried approaching the subject from several angles by asking more questions, thinking maybe I could get a better answer. But a better answer didn't come. When I eventually explained that we could *not* proceed toward membership, she began to cry. I wanted to cry, too. If you had heard her tough life story, you would have felt the same way. But it would not have shown love to her or to the church to proceed.

So I invited her to meet with a woman in the church to walk through the Gospel of Mark in six sessions. She accepted. She met with the woman. Several weeks later, we sat down again and started all over. This time, she explained the gospel wonderfully and joined our church. "To the nations: Look here! Another representative!"

I guess you could describe what I did as making her "jump through a hoop." I hope instead you would call it pastoring her and helping to make sure she knew the gospel and was converted, not to mention caring for the church and the reputation of Christ.

FAITH

I said church membership begins when a church affirms a person's profession of faith, as Jesus did with Peter. To facilitate this process, churches often use a statement of faith to ensure that everyone having the conversation is saying and believing the same things.

For instance, the Mormons, the Jehovah's Witnesses, and some liberal Protestants would confess their belief in Jesus, just as Peter did. But they wouldn't say that Jesus is God. So which Jesus are we talking about? A church's statement of faith helps to clarify.

In the early church, some denied that Jesus was fully human. Listen to how the apostle John encourages one church to be discriminating in this matter:

> Dear friends, do not believe every spirit, but test the spirits to see whether they are from God, because many false prophets have gone out into the world. This is how you can recognize the Spirit of God: Every spirit that acknowledges that Jesus Christ has come in the flesh is from God, but every spirit that does not acknowledge Jesus is not from God. (1 John 4:1–3)

There were prophets who said, "Yeah, I believe in Jesus, too. I'm just like you." But John said, "You need to probe a little. They might not be just like you."

Two thousand years have passed, and false teaching has only proliferated. That's why most churches have statements of faith that address God, Scripture, sin, salvation, the church, and Jesus's return.

The goal in asking a person to affirm a statement of faith is not to affirm professional theologians, it's to affirm Christians. Listen to Jesus's standards: "Whoever humbles himself like this child is the greatest in the kingdom of heaven. Whoever receives one such child in my name receives me" (Matt. 18:4–5 ESV). In other words, churches should tune their ears for a Spirit-given brokenness and humility before God. What does such brokenness sound like? It sounds something like this: "Yes, I'm a rotten sinner. Yes, God should judge me. But yes! Jesus died on the cross for my sins. Now he's my Lord and I'm following him."

What does a broken heart sound like? It sounds like the

beginning of good doctrine and like a heart that trusts what the Bible says about God and about us.

REPENTANCE

Christianity doesn't only begin with faith. Therefore neither does church membership. Both begin with repentance. Jesus preached, "The kingdom of God is at hand; repent and believe in the gospel" (Mark 1:15 ESV).

Like good doctrine and faith, repentance is the fruit of a Spirit-broken heart.

If I really were to write a standards guide for those conducting membership interviews, I would go straight to Matthew's beatitudes. It might read something like this:

> Look for the ones who are poor in spirit; who mourn their sin; who aren't entitled, always insisting on their own way, but are meek; who are sick to death of sin and all its nonsense and so hunger and thirst for righteousness like it is water. When you find people like that, make sure they know who Jesus is. Make sure Jesus is the one who fills their impoverished spirit, who has forgiven their sins, who receives their life and worship, and whose righteousness they depend upon and pursue. When you find such people, tell them to join!

Notice that it's not a person's moral perfection that qualifies him or her for church membership. It's just the opposite. It's his or her recognition of a lack of moral perfection coupled with a hunger for it. It's not the people who never sin; it's the people who fight against sin. A church's judicial work is to affirm not the righteous but the unrighteous who thirst for righteousness—the righteousness only God in Christ can give.

Here's one more way to say it: what makes people acceptable to a church is not their own moral purity, but Christ's—not what they have done to save themselves, but what God has done to save them.

BAPTISM

Do people really need to sit down in a church office with an elder for an interview before joining a church? No, there are different ways to make sure someone represents Jesus before placing the church's stamp of approval on them. We'll think about this further in chapter 8.

What's important to see now is that there *is* one matter that churches should require of its members beyond salvation, and that's baptism. We saw in chapter 2 that the first step of the Christian life in the New Testament is baptism—always. The crowds asked Peter what to do to be saved, and he answered, "Repent and be baptized" (Acts 2:38). Paul, writing to the Roman church, simply assumed that all of them had been baptized (Rom. 6:4). And it's the first thing Jesus commands his disciples to do when making disciples (Matt. 28:19).

Baptism does not save a person, but Jesus means for his saved individuals to publicly identify with him and his people. It's one piece of how his citizens become official. It's how they wave the flag.

In the same way, churches have for two thousand years treated baptism as a prerequisite for membership. Does the Bible say, "You must be baptized before joining a church"? No, but it does say, "Repent and be baptized." If you want to identify yourself with Christ's people and expect them to identify with you, you need to first identify yourself with Christ, which is the purpose of baptism. To refuse baptism would seem, well, unrepentant. As Mark Dever has put it, getting wet is the easiest command Jesus ever gave to follow. It only gets harder from there.

CONCLUSION

A pastor friend phoned me several weeks ago and asked if he should let a certain man rejoin his church. This man had resigned his membership several months prior but now wanted to come back. He was a slightly troublesome individual, not blatantly divisive, but immature and occasionally vexing to the leadership. My friend was thinking about not letting the man rejoin.

I asked him if he thought the man was a Christian. "Yes," came the slow and slightly reluctant answer.

I asked him if he would be willing to stand up in a crowded mall, point to this man, and tell everyone that he was a representative of Jesus. "I suppose," came an even more reluctant answer.

"Well, then I think you may need to let him join again. We have to let the jerk Christians join our churches, too."

Churches must not look for the people who are never jerks, but for the people who admit that they are jerks and are willing to fight it.

Kind of like me. Maybe like you?

6

HOW DOES A CHRISTIAN SUBMIT TO A CHURCH? (BEING A MEMBER)

Earlier I said that Christians don't really join churches, they submit to them. After all, Jesus has given churches authority to bind and loose on earth, which means Christians are called to submit to them as an act of submission to him. It's like a child who honors God by honoring his or her parents.

The word *submit* scares most people today, in part because we have seen so much leadership abused, including leadership in churches. Still, throughout Scripture God reveals that he means authority for our good. The Author of creation used his authority to create and bless us. In the same way, he means for his authorized human stewards to use their authority to author life and prosperity in others (for instance, read 2 Sam. 23:3–4; also, Isa. 11:2–10).

What then does it mean to submit to a church, and is it for our good?

STARRY NIGHT

To answer these questions, let's start by getting into a car and driving to Arizona.

I once went camping in the desert of Arizona just a short distance from the Grand Canyon. The first night we laid out our sleeping bags under the stars. I have never seen anything like it. Out in the clear desert air, the stars shone so brightly you could hold out your hand and almost see its shadow on the ground.

That sky is what I want you to see. I want you to look up and see a black canvas peppered with ten thousand diamonds of light.

Why? This is the picture Paul paints of Christians and churches in the world. He told the Christians in the ancient city of Philippi that he wanted them to

> become blameless and pure,
> "children of God without fault in a warped and crooked generation."
> Then you will shine among them like stars in the sky. (Phil. 2:15)

The city of Philippi was that dark canvas. The Christians were to be the diamonds of light. The city was crooked and depraved. The Christians were to be blameless and pure.

Can you see it? Paul wanted these believers to shine, and for them to shine in their homes and workplaces, in the market and on the playing field.

But here's something you must not miss about what Paul was saying. He didn't just want them to glow and sparkle when they were spread out, separated from one another. He wanted them to shine *through their lives together*.

I showed you the one verse about stars shining. But pull the camera back. A few paragraphs before this verse Paul told his readers that he wanted them to live a life "worthy of the gospel" (Phil. 1:27). What does a life that is worthy of the gospel look like?

Helpfully, Paul painted two pictures of such a worthy life for the Philippians. Picture one was what he wanted to see in the Philippian church itself. He told them to stand firm in "one Spirit," to contend for the gospel as "one," to be "like-minded," to share "the same love," to be "one in spirit and of one mind" (Phil. 1:27–2:2).

It's a monochrome picture, isn't it? Their life together is to be the color of unity. And they are to paint in the color of unity through submitting to one another. Paul goes on to command them, "Do nothing out of selfish ambition or vain conceit." Instead, he says, "In humility value others above yourselves," and "not looking to your own interests but each of you to the interests of the others" (Phil. 2:3–4). The picture of unity, in other words, is a picture of mutual submission.

Before Paul finishes this first picture, however, he interrupts himself and paints a second picture of submission, one that was to be a model for the first. When it comes to all this unity and submission and love, Paul said, "Have the same mindset as Christ Jesus." Christ Jesus was "in very nature God," but he "made himself nothing by taking the very nature of a servant, being made in human likeness." What's more, "he humbled himself by becoming obedient to death—even death on a cross!" Wonderfully, God therefore "exalted him to the highest place and gave him the name that is above every name" (Phil. 2:5–9).

Do you see the connection between the two pictures? This second picture is a picture of the gospel—Christ becoming man, being crucified, and rising from the dead. Christ did what only he could do: pay for sin and defeat death. The first picture is of a life *worthy* of this gospel. It's a life devoted to submissive love and humble unity among Christ's people.

Paul is basically saying, "Do you want to know how a gospel professor should live among other Christians? Just look at your Savior!"

At this point in the letter, Paul returns to his first picture. He tells them to continue obeying. To work out their salvation with fear and trembling. To do everything without complaining or arguing. And to be blameless and pure. Then they will "shine like stars in the . . . sky" (Phil. 2:12–16).

When Christians pursue unity in their churches by submitting to one another, then their churches will glow like porch lights on a dark city street, like lanterns in the nighttime woods.

That is a life worthy of the gospel and a church worthy of the gospel.

If you know how dark and lost this world is, you can see what a beautiful picture it is. You know the broken marriages, the racial injustice, the abandoned children, the many kinds of addictions that enslave people. You've seen the loneliness and hurt and anxiety. You've experienced rage, hatred, pride, as well as the self-deceit and self-justification that accompanies all such things. Some of these things you've seen in others; some you've seen in yourself.

Ah, but to hold out these glowing lanterns of light to the dark world! Isn't that what you want our churches to be and to do?

EIGHT WAYS TO SUBMIT TO A LOCAL CHURCH

Paul looked right into the eyes of the Philippian church and told them to submit to one another's good, just as Christ had submitted himself for their good.

The same is true for us and our local churches. Just as Christ submitted his whole life for our good, so we should submit our whole lives for one another's good. It's not as if there is some area of our life that is exempt from considering the interests of others better than our own. Specifically, we should give ourselves to our churches publicly, physically, socially, affectionately, financially, vocationally, ethically, and spiritually.

Publicly

First, Christians should submit to their local churches publicly, by which I mean formally or officially. They should join a church by committing to the local body of believers where they will regularly receive the Lord's Supper. Jesus publicly identified himself with his church. We should publicly identify with him and his people as well—by joining a church. (See chapter 8 for what this might mean for the persecuted church.)

Physically/Geographically

Second, Christians should submit to their local churches physically and perhaps geographically. We submit physically by gathering regularly with the church. "Let us . . . not [give] up meeting together, as some are in the habit of doing," the author of the Hebrews says (Heb. 10:25; also, Acts 2:42–47). Meet every Lord's Day (Acts 20:7; 1 Cor. 16:2).

Now, let me raise the stakes a little. If you *can*, "consider others better than yourselves" and "look to the interests of others" by living geographically close to the church. When a person lives within walking distance of a church or clumps of members, it's easier to invite people to one's house for dinner, to watch one another's children while running errands, to pick up bread or milk at the store for one another. In other words, it's just plain easier to integrate daily life when there is relative—even walkable—geographic proximity.

When considering what home to buy or apartment to rent, Christians do well to ask some of the same questions that non-Christians ask (How much does it cost? Are there good schools nearby?). But Christians also do well to ask additional questions like these:

- Will the mortgage or rent payment allow for generosity to others?
- Will it give other church members quick access to me for discipleship and hospitality?

During my family's last move, the question of submitting geographically to the church came down to a choice between two houses, both of which were affordable, but very different otherwise. House One was newer, better designed, more attractive, did not need repairs, and was less expensive. But it was thirty minutes' drive from the church building and near no church members. House Two was older, draftier, in need of several repairs such as a rotting front porch and an occasionally flooding basement, and was more expensive. But it was only a fifteen-minute drive from the church building and, more importantly, within walkable proximity of a dozen (now two dozen) church families. I sought the counsel of several elders, all of whom advised me to prioritize church relationships. This actually meant choosing the older, less attractive, more expensive house.

Gratefully, we did, and how enriching it's been for our whole family! My wife interacts with the other mothers almost daily. And our children with their children. I met with one brother every weekday morning to pray and read Scripture for a year and a half. And our church families can work together in serving and evangelizing our neighbors.

Must a Christian move close to other members of his or her church? No, the Bible doesn't command this. But it's one concrete way to love your church.

Did Jesus submit himself physically and geographically for our good? He left heaven!

Socially

Third, we should submit ourselves socially. Churches should be more than social clubs, but they shouldn't be less. Our friends are the ones we imitate and follow. We spend money where they spend money. We raise our children like they raise their children. We pray like they pray. Our friends form who we become as we imitate one another (see James 4:4; also 1 Cor. 15:33).

The local church community should be a place where Christians form and shape one another for good through all the dynamics of friendship. Christian friends are surely valuable inside or outside the same local church. But friends within a local church will be formed by the same ministry of the Word, giving them the opportunity to extend that ministry more carefully into one another's lives throughout the week.

Also, the church should be a safe place to move outside our social comfort zones. Friendships should form between old and young, rich and poor, uneducated and educated, one ethnic group and another.

Have you ever heard a voice inside your head saying, "But I don't want to be friends with him. He's not like me. We have different backgrounds. We're not interested in the same things"? I sure have. But consider how Paul might respond: Jesus did not consider equality with God something to be grasped, but made himself nothing. He was God—not like you! Then he became human—like you!

In the same humility, consider others better than yourself when it comes to picking your friends. Look to their interests, not your own.

Affectionately

One component of friendship, of course, is the sharing of affections. Christians should submit their affections to one another. What gives me joy or grief? What is it that causes me to celebrate or mourn?

Listen to what Paul says to the Corinthians: "Have equal concern for each other. If one part suffers, every part suffers with it; if one part is honored, every part rejoices with it" (1 Cor. 12:25b–26).

To the Romans he says, "Be devoted to one another in love. Honor one another above yourselves" (Rom. 12:10).

He commands us to rejoice with the brother who gets a big job promotion and all the money and prestige that come with it. Can we? He commands the thirty-year-old single woman who longs for marriage to rejoice with the twenty-two-year-old woman when she marries. Can she? Can the poor man mourn with the rich man when he loses his job? Saying yes to these questions—rather than saying yes to "selfish ambition and vain conceit"—requires something more than sentiment. It requires a heart to be altered by the gospel and the Spirit.

Fulfilling Paul's command to "value others better than yourselves" with "the same love" means knowing the love of him who did not consider equality with God something to be grasped, and then loving like him.

Financially

Christians should submit themselves to their local churches financially. This will look different from context to context. But however it's done, Christians should look for ways to fulfill biblical commands like these:

- "Share with the Lord's people who are in need. Practice hospitality" (Rom. 12:13; also Gal. 2:10; 1 John 3:17).
- "Now about the collection for the Lord's people: Do what I told the Galatian churches to do. On the first day of every week, each one of you should set aside a sum of money in keeping with your income, saving it up, so that when I come no collections will have to be made" (1 Cor. 16:1–2; Rom. 15:26).
- "The Lord has commanded that those who preach the gospel should receive their living from the gospel" (1 Cor. 9:14, also 9:11–13; Matt. 10:10; Luke 10:7; Gal. 6:6; also 1 Tim. 5:17–18).

Vocationally

Christians should submit their vocations to their churches. For some people, this means going into vocational ministry. For every Christian, this means recognizing that the lives of our fellow members will stretch on for eternity, while our jobs will not.

I know men and women in secular employment who, for the sake of serving in their local churches, have turned down promotions and more money, who have moved from larger, more reputable firms to smaller ones, who have refused to move to another city. In each case, the individual turned down the opportunity because he or she knew it would have hindered the ability to care for the church and family. I have also known others who refused to work on Sundays or have quit jobs when required to, not because they are Sabbatarians, but because that's when the church gathers.

By the way, some of the best nonstaff elders in a church are not the men who move up the professional ladder but the men who are willing to move down it for the sake of the church.

Ethically

Christians should submit themselves to their local churches ethically. This does not mean making the church an absolute authority any more than a child should regard his or her parents this way. Rather, Christians should look to the church for ethical instruction, counsel, accountability, and discipline in matters that are addressed by God's Word.

Paul writes, "Brothers, if anyone is caught in any transgression, you who are spiritual should restore him in a spirit of gentleness. Keep watch on yourself, lest you too be tempted" (Gal. 6:1 ESV). Jude says to "save others by snatching them out of the fire" (Jude 23 ESV). The local church is the primary place where we seek to help other believers fight against their sin and where we, in turn, should open ourselves up to receive the same help.

If a brother sins against you, go and show him his fault (Matt. 18:15). If he listens, you have won your brother. If he doesn't, take two or three others. If he doesn't listen to them, take it to the church (Matt. 18:16–17).

All this is part of what it means to submit to one's local church ethically.

Spiritually

Finally, Christians should submit themselves to a local church spiritually. By this I mean three specific things:

- First, this community is where we should seek to exercise our spiritual gifts. Paul observes that "to each is given the manifestation of the Spirit for the common good" (1 Cor. 12:7 ESV).
- Second, the local church is the community where Christians should build one another up in the faith through God's Word. Jude writes, "But you, beloved, building yourselves up in your most holy faith and praying in the Holy Spirit, keep yourselves in the love of God, waiting for the mercy of our Lord Jesus Christ that leads to eternal life" (Jude 20–21 ESV; also Eph. 4:11–32; Heb. 10:25).
- Third, it's the people for whom we should intercede regularly in our prayers.

SUBMITTING TO UGLINESS

Truth be told, people are not afraid to submit. They just want to submit to beauty, like the valiant hero who submits himself to rescuing the damsel in distress.

What's unexpected about Christianity is that its hero doesn't risk all for a damsel but for what the Bible likens to a harlot. Then he calls everyone that he saves to submit themselves to this same harlot—the bride still being made ready, the church.

Now, submitting to ugliness does scare people. And that's what submitting to the local church can be. Churches are filled with other sinners whose visions of glory contradict our own. But this is how Christ loved us: "Just as I have loved you, you also are to love one another" (John 13:34 ESV).

Christ's love wonderfully transforms the ugly into the beautiful (see Eph. 5:22–31). Our love for one another should do the same thing—help the ugly become beautiful.

Who can love in this way? Only the ones whose eyes have been opened and whose hearts have been freed from the slavery of loving this world: "So if the Son sets you free, you will be free indeed" (John 8:36 ESV).

How Should Members Relate to Pastors?

Every church member will stand before God's throne and give an account for how he or she worked to protect the gospel in the lives of his or her fellow members (see Galatians 1). That said, the Holy Spirit has made pastors and elders the overseers of the church (Acts 20:28; Titus 1:7; 1 Pet. 5:2). That means pastors or elders represent the church's work of oversight in the day-to-day life of the congregation. Submitting to the church often means submitting to them. Broadly speaking, how should members relate to pastors?

1. *Members should formally affirm their pastors.* Different traditions disagree on this, but I believe that since Christians are ultimately responsible before God for what they are taught (see Galatians 1), church members are responsible for choosing their leaders. Congregations should let elders lead in this process, but the final affirmation is the church's. (It may also be the case that the church's authority to affirm its leaders is an apostolic authority, which it inherits through the apostolic keys. See Acts 14:23; see also the congregation's role in Acts 1 and Acts 6.)

2. *Members should honor their pastors.* Our culture's ability to understand honoring seems to be diminishing continually. But just as the Bible calls children to honor their parents, so Christians should honor their pastors. The Bible even says to give them "double honor" (1 Tim. 5:17). And this includes paying them (5:18).

3. *Members should submit to their pastors.* These two verses in Hebrews need to be incorporated into our understanding of the Christian life: "Remember your leaders, who spoke the word of God to you. Consider the outcome of their way of life and imitate their faith" (Heb. 13:7). "Have confidence in your leaders and submit to their authority, because they keep watch over you as those who must give an account. Do this so that their work will be a joy, not a burden, for that would be of no benefit to you" (Heb. 13:17).

4. *Members should pray for their pastors.* These men are the ones whose lives and teaching help to sustain the church. Will it not benefit us to pray for them?

5. *Members should bring charges against disqualified pastors.* Since they are out front, Paul protects leaders by requiring two or three witnesses to level a charge against them (1 Tim. 5:19). That said, the congregation *should not* allow an elder who has disqualified himself to continue serving.

6. *Members should fire gospel-denying pastors.* When false teachers entered the Galatian church, Paul did not correct the elders. He corrected the church. When pastors begin to deny the gospel or teach other heresies, God calls church members to fire them.

7

WHAT HAPPENS WHEN MEMBERS DON'T REPRESENT JESUS?

If you were to visit your local library and open the first regular edition of *U.S. News & World Report* published after September 11, 2001, you would find the photograph of a man sitting on the steps of the US Capitol Building and holding an American flag.[1] His name is Hermono or Mono for short. Mono has no last name, so the space for a last name on his American driver's license reads "Lnu," which stands for "last name unknown." Mono is a citizen of Indonesia, but he is a die-hard American patriot.

Mono had been in America for several years when a Christian named Doug encountered him on the Mall in Washington, DC. It was July 4, 2001, and Mono was enjoying the fireworks. Doug had other plans. He shared the gospel with Mono. Mono, remarkably, heard and believed. He was born again.

Several months later, my church baptized him and made

him a member. It was official. Alert the press, and tell the nations: here was a new citizen of Christ's kingdom.

The church enjoyed Mono's enthusiasm, kindness, and generosity. On one occasion, he purchased a set of dinnerware just so that he could host a dinner for all the men in the church who had impacted his discipleship to Christ. He loved the church, and the church loved him.

Sometime that fall, after joining the church, the elders learned that Mono was working in the country illegally. He had lied to them about his work status, and he was continuing to lie to his employer, who believed that he was legal. Opinions were mixed about how to respond to the illegal immigration status since the US government was not enforcing the pertinent laws. But one thing was clear: Christians must not lie to their employers by falsifying their employment status. Jesus does not lie, much less persist in lying—nor should his representatives.

For months the church pleaded with Mono to come clean. It tried to help him financially. Still, he refused. Sometimes it looked as if he would relent, but then he clamped down again, resolved to remain in America at all costs. It began to seem as though he prized America more than the Word of God.

Finally, with broken hearts, the church disciplined or excommunicated Mono for refusing to tell the truth. They told him that they could no longer call him a Christian and affirm his citizenship in the kingdom. They instructed him to stop receiving the Lord's Supper. They removed him from membership.

It was a sad day for the church.

WHAT IS CHURCH DISCIPLINE?

What is church discipline? In broad terms, church discipline is one part of the discipleship process, the part where we correct sin and point the disciple toward the better path. To be *discipled* is, among other things, to be *disciplined*. And a Christian is disciplined through instruction and correction, as in a math class where the teacher teaches the lesson and then corrects the students' errors. Informally, then, church discipline begins with a private word of admonition to a brother who is sinning.

In more specific and formal terms, church discipline is the act of removing an individual from membership and participation in the Lord's Table. The church is not telling the individual to stop attending its public gatherings. The church wants the person to come and hear God's Word preached. Rather, the church is saying that it can no longer affirm the person's profession of faith, and so it refuses to give the Lord's Supper. It's excommunicating, or ex-communion-ing, the person.

In addition to Matthew 18 (see chapter 3), perhaps the most well-known passage on church discipline is 1 Corinthians 5. There, Paul rebukes the Corinthian church for being "proud" of tolerating a man who "is sleeping with his father's wife." He tells them to "put out of your fellowship" this man (1 Cor. 5:2), to "judge" him (1 Cor. 5:12), to "expel" him (1 Cor. 5:13), to "hand this man over to Satan" (1 Cor. 5:5) that is, the kingdom of Satan, which is the world. He can no longer be regarded as a citizen of God's kingdom, not when he is living like this.

Remember, to be a church member is to be a Jesus

representative. Discipline, then, is the appropriate course of action when the character of a person's representation brings shame on Jesus's name.

WHAT'S THE PURPOSE OF CHURCH DISCIPLINE?

Church discipline has at least five purposes. First, discipline aims *to expose*. Sin, like cancer, loves to hide. Discipline exposes the cancer so that it might be cut out quickly (see 1 Cor. 5:2).

Second, discipline aims *to warn*. A church does not enact God's judgment through discipline. Rather, it stages a small play that pictures the great judgment to come (1 Cor. 5:5).

Third, it aims *to save*. Churches pursue discipline when they see a member taking the path toward death, and none of their pleading and arm waving causes the person to turn around. It's the device of last resort (1 Cor. 5:5).

Fourth, discipline aims *to protect*. Just as cancer spreads from one cell to another, so sin quickly spreads from one person to another (1 Cor. 5:6).

Fifth, it aims *to present a good witness for Jesus*. Church discipline, strange to say, is actually good for non-Christians, because it helps to preserve the attractive distinctiveness of God's people (see 1 Cor. 5:1). Churches, remember, are to be salt and light. "But if the salt loses its saltiness," Jesus said, "it is no longer good for anything, except to be thrown out and trampled underfoot" (Matt. 5:13).

Mono hid his sin in the dark. He didn't want the lie exposed. And when it was exposed, he didn't want to treat it like sin. He wanted to treat it as "inevitable" or "necessary" or "not that bad." But he was self-deceived by a heart that was craving something more than Jesus and his Word.

The church, lovingly, did not want him or others to be deceived. The church wanted to warn him, to save him, to protect young believers who might be tempted to defend lying as reasonable, and to love its neighbors by preserving the church's distinctness.

Therefore, the church, through discipline, exposed his true love by handing him over to his own choices. In the end, the church did nothing more or less than declare, "You're not choosing Jesus, so you must not be with Jesus."

The underlying purpose in every act of discipline, of course, must be love: *love for the individual, love for the church, love for the watching world, love for Christ.*

God, after all, "disciplines the one he loves"; and "he chastens everyone he accepts as his son" (Heb. 12:6). By abstaining from discipline, we claim that we love better than God.

God lovingly knows that discipline yields life, growth, and health: "God disciplines us for our good, in order that we may share in his holiness" (Heb. 12:10). Yes, it's painful, but it pays off: "No discipline seems pleasant at the time, but painful. Later on, however, it produces a harvest of righteousness and peace for those who have been trained by it" (Heb. 12:11).

WHEN SHOULD A CHURCH PRACTICE CHURCH DISCIPLINE?

The short answer is, a church should practice church discipline when someone sins. Church members should learn the skill of how to privately and tenderly confront sin. That doesn't mean you raise the hammer and whack a brother every time he commits the slightest infraction. Often it's best to say nothing. And when you do say something, it is typically best to begin by asking questions, making sure you have the facts right and are giving the person the benefit of the doubt. Still, churches should cultivate the kinds of relationships where informal correction is invited and received—as an act of love.

Formal church discipline from the entire congregation is reserved for sins of such significance that the church no longer feels able to affirm a person's profession of faith. The person continues to call himself or herself a Christian and a Jesus representative, but his or her words are no longer believable because of the nature of the sin.

Let me put it this way: somewhere there's a line between sins and sin patterns that you expect of Christians and sins and sin patterns that make you think someone may not be a Christian. Church discipline is warranted, you might say, when an individual crosses from the first domain into the second. It's not the kind of thing that just gets under your skin personally; it's the kind of thing that a whole assembly of people looks at and agrees is disqualifying. The person's words can no longer be trusted. His profession has lost its credibility. He might claim to be "repentant" or "just fine" or "not disobeying *that* bad," but for whatever reason the church can no longer believe him. So the church removes its public affirmation by barring him from the Lord's Table. It takes away his passport and announces that it can no longer formally affirm his citizenship in Christ's kingdom.

One might say, for instance, there's a difference between the occasional lie which is repented of and a lie on which a person builds a life and refuses to relinquish. The latter characterized Mono.

Does this mean that churches must know people's hearts? Of course not. God has not given us X-ray eyes. But God does call churches to consider the fruit of individual lives and make a judgment call (Paul uses exactly this word—1 Cor. 5:12; cf. Matt. 3:8; 7:16–20; 12:33; 21:43).

Can we say anything more concrete about where this line between one domain and the other exists? I believe we can say that formal church discipline is required in cases of *outward*, *serious*, and *unrepentant* sin. First, a sin must have an *outward* manifestation. Churches should not throw the red flag of ejection every time they suspect greed or pride in someone's heart. It must be something that can be seen with the eyes or heard with the ears.

Second, a sin must be *serious*. Not every sin should be pursued to the utmost. There needs to be some place in a church's life for love to cover "a multitude of sins" (1 Peter 4:8). Thankfully, God does not perceptibly discipline us every time we sin.

Finally, a sin must be *unrepentant*. The person involved has been confronted with God's commands in Scripture, but he or she refuses to let go of the sin. From all appearances, the person prizes the sin more than Jesus.

Now, there are some instances when a person might apologize and claim to be repentant, but a church might legitimately decide to proceed with discipline anyway. I believe this is acceptable when, for some reason or another, the church simply cannot believe the person's words. Maybe the person is characterized by habitual lying. Maybe the sin is so deliberate (like a long pattern of abuse or premeditated murder) or heinous (like rape) that any quick words of apology remain unbelievable. It's not that such sins cannot be forgiven, it's just that some time needs to pass and the fruit of repentance displayed before a church can responsibly pronounce forgiveness (see the example in Acts 8:17–24). On the other hand, when a church becomes convinced that a person is genuinely repentant, it should not proceed with formal discipline (and I cannot think of a single exception to this principle).

HOW SHOULD A CHURCH PRACTICE CHURCH DISCIPLINE?

Matthew 18 describes the basic process of church discipline, moving from one person, to several, to the whole church. Jesus's basic concern here is to extend the process no wider than necessary for producing reconciliation.

Sometimes the processes of discipline should move quite slowly, as when the individual shows interest in fighting the sin. Sometimes the processes of discipline need to speed up, as in 1 Corinthians 5 where the man's sin is flagrant and apparently unrepentant.

Also, it's not just the nature of the sin that needs to be considered, it's the nature of the sinner himself. Different sinners, to put it bluntly, require different strategies (1 Thess. 5:14).

Church members often wonder how to interact with someone who has been disciplined. The New Testament addresses this matter in a number of places (1 Cor. 5:9, 11; 2 Thess. 3:6, 14–15; 2 Tim. 3:5; Titus 3:10; 2 John 10). The basic counsel the elders of my own church give is that the general tenor of one's relationships with the disciplined individual should markedly change. Interactions should not be characterized by casualness but by deliberate conversations about repentance. Certainly family members should continue to fulfill family obligations (see Eph. 6:1–3; 1 Tim. 5:8; 1 Pet. 3:1–2).

When does restoration to the church's fellowship occur? When the sinner repents. Sometimes repentance is black and white, as with a man who has abandoned his wife. He must return. Sometimes it is gray, as with a person caught in a cycle of addiction, and much wisdom is needed.

Once a church decides to restore a repenting individual to its fellowship and the Lord's Table, there should be no talk of a probation period or second-class citizenship. Rather the church should publicly pronounce its forgiveness (John 20:23), affirm its love for the repenting individual (2 Cor. 2:8), and celebrate (Luke 15:24).

WISER THAN MAN'S WISDOM

When churches start to practice discipline, they will often find themselves facing complex situations with no exact case study in Scripture to follow. But the church's uppermost concern must be to guard the reputation of Christ. It does this by carefully considering whether it can continue to affirm the verbal profession of someone whose life grossly mischaracterizes Christ. Guarding his reputation is, in fact, what's most loving for the sinner, the church, and the nations.

It proved to be most loving for Mono and for the nation of Indonesia. Sometime after his excommunication, Mono felt convicted of his sin, bought a plane ticket, and returned to Indonesia. About a year later, he wrote this e-mail to one of my church's pastors:

> Andy, thank you for this very encouraging e-mail you wrote. Thank you to the church for always remembering me and for continuing to pray for me. I have to confess, I left the church with an unfinished sinful matter, and the sad thing is I took it lightly. I should have learned to humble myself and come to you for reconciliation. Are we enemies to each other? No, we are Christian brothers. I was too proud and stubborn. My pride led me to think that God alone would settle the matter without me taking some action. Then I went on with my own way. And the result? I did not find a peace. . . . I know now why God brought me home, because there an eternal prize for me awaited. I wish I can describe to you what kind of relationship I have today with Him. It is too beautiful to describe. . . . Andy, I have been praying for this reconciliation to happen, but please show me how to do it. I am longing to reunite with my family again. Lastly please send my thank you to the church members and to the elders, and I miss you all.
>
> Much love,
> Mono

And it was with joy that our church sent the following reply:

> Mono,
> It's been great to get back in touch with you. I wanted to let you know that last night at the church members meeting

we shared with the membership part of your recent e-mail. . . . Everyone was humbled and encouraged by your words and your actions.

The membership voted unanimously to affirm the following motion from the elders:

Motion: The CHBC elders happily recommend that the members of CHBC acknowledge with thankfulness to God the repentance of our brother, Mono, that we formally express to him our forgiveness for his actions toward us, and that we publicly renew our expression of fellowship with him and love for him as our brother in Christ. And we do all this with great thanks to God for his faithfulness to his Word and to those who honor it by their obedience.

Then we prayed for you as a congregation asking God's richest blessings on you and on your life and work.

May God continue to encourage and sustain you as you follow after him.

Your brother in Christ,

Andy

Mono now serves as an evangelist among a Muslim people group in Indonesia.

So the church acted, Mono repented, God was glorified, and now a nation on the opposite side of the planet is reaping the benefit.

Is not the foolishness of God wiser than man's wisdom?

Jesus reigns.

When You Should Not Submit

All of us, at times, will be called to endure humbly a leader's mistakes and sins. Nonetheless, should you find yourself in a church where the leadership is characteristically abusive, I would, in most cases, encourage you to flee. Flee to protect your discipleship, to protect your family, to set a good example for the members left behind, and to serve non-Christian neighbors by not lending credibility to the church's ministry.

How do you recognize abusive leadership? Paul requires two witnesses for a charge to be leveled against an elder (1 Tim. 5:19), probably because he knows that leaders will be charged with infelicities more than others, often unfairly. That said, abusive churches and Christian leaders *characteristically*

- Make dogmatic prescriptions in places where Scripture is silent.
- Rely on intelligence, humor, charm, guilt, emotions, or threats rather than on God's Word and prayer (see Acts 6:4).
- Play favorites.
- Punish those who disagree.
- Employ extreme forms of communication (tempers, silent treatment).

- Recommend courses of action that always, somehow, improve the leader's own situation, even at the expense of others.
- Speak often and quickly.
- Seldom do good deeds in secret.
- Seldom encourage.
- Seldom give the benefit of the doubt.
- Emphasize outward conformity, rather than repentance of heart.
- Preach, counsel, disciple, and oversee the church with lips that fail to ground everything in what Christ has done in the gospel and to give glory to God.

8

MUST MEMBERSHIP LOOK THE SAME EVERYWHERE?

The church has no name. It has no building. And it is not registered with the city because the government would shut it down if it knew it existed.

It meets in a member's home in a central Asian city where almost everyone is Muslim. It has eight to ten members, and it will never grow beyond twenty. When it does, it will have to divide itself. Houses are too small, and, more importantly, Christians in this country need to fly under the radar screen of the city authorities and Muslim clerics.

The church gathers every Sunday with its two elders, "Frank" and "Hanz," in order to pray, sing, and learn from the Bible. Both men converted within the last decade and learned most of what they know about the Bible from two or three missionaries.

The question we want to ask in this chapter is, should the way Frank and Hanz's church practices membership look the same as a church in a populous Western city like Washington, DC, where I attend church? Must membership look the same everywhere?

HOW MEMBERSHIP IS THE SAME EVERYWHERE

The basic answer is, yes and no. Let's start with the yes. Membership will look the same everywhere because the Jesus-established local church *is* its membership. And Jesus has given every church everywhere *the same tools* for accomplishing *the same task*.

- The task: to be a distinct, marked-off society that, through its very distinctness, blesses the nations and garners praise for the heavenly Father (Matt. 5:3–16).
- The tools: the authority to guard the gospel, to affirm credible professions of gospel faith, to oversee Christian discipleship, to teach disciples everything he's commanded, and to exclude false professors (Matt. 16:13–19; 18:15–20; 28:18–20).

Furthermore, membership will look the same everywhere because all churches dwell *in precisely the same context*: enemy territory. Local churches, remember, are embassies. They don't dwell in neutral or friendly territory but behind enemy lines. That's why Paul in 1 Corinthians 5 equates excommunicating the man caught in adultery with handing him over to Satan. Satan is the prince of this world, and the kingdoms of the world temporarily belong to him (John 12:31; 14:30; Matt. 4:8–9).

Now, Satan uses different devices in different locations to undermine Christ's kingdom. A favorite device of his in the West is cultural Christianity. The American brand of cultural Christianity results from well-intending adults handing out the candy of cheap grace to five-year-olds and twenty-five-year-olds alike. You ask them if they want to be with mommy and daddy in heaven or pressure them into walking an aisle. The point is, you play on their fears, emotions, or appetites in order to get quick, unconsidered professions of faith. Then you immediately affirm those professions. The European state-church brand, on the other hand, is much more civilized. Cheap grace comes with a birth certificate.

The genius of this device in both locations is that it allows Satan to inoculate their hosts against real Christianity. It's nearly impossible to share the gospel with a cultural Christian because he already gives lip service to it. "Yes, I believe *that*." But there's no repentance. He merely baptizes a slightly sanitized version of his old self into Christianity.

The other big danger of cultural Christianity is that it fools churches into thinking that they don't live in enemy territory. Churches feel as though their nation is home. That it's safe.

On the other hand, Satan uses very different devices in different lands. In Orissa, India, he will use a technically illegal Hindu mob to burn down a church. In the central Asian city where Frank and Hanz pastor, he will use the local authorities themselves to infiltrate church gatherings, confiscate materials, and imprison the pastors. In parts of Africa he will use ancestor worship and African traditional religion to join forces with the gospel and morph it into something different.

Since human beings live in physical bodies, our eyes tend to fix themselves on surface-level differences. But the most important things are never seen with the eyes, and for our purposes here, the most important thing to realize is that every church everywhere dwells in hostile territory. There will be no holy land or holy building on the planet until Jesus comes back.

No matter where you go, no matter what year it is, the local church protects the gospel against all kinds of attack by taking great care in who it receives as a member. Every church must ask these basic questions: Who do you say that Jesus is? Are you sure you're really ready to take up your cross and give yourself to identifying with him and his body?

HOW MEMBERSHIP IS DIFFERENT EVERYWHERE

At the same time, it should be clear from what I have already said that churches in different locations face different challenges. The basic task and the tools are the same, but the structures or strategies might look a little different.

Societal Complexity

To begin with, the larger and more complex a society becomes, the more difficult it is to affirm and oversee credible professions of faith. This work is made difficult by job transience, social mobility, church size, urban sprawl, demanding work schedules, religious pluralism, ethnic prejudice, multi-denominationalism, centuries of accumulated heresies, false churches, church hopping, cultural trends such as individualism and consumerism, and much more. The bigger and more a complex society becomes, the harder it is to know who's with whom.

Are you with Jesus? I can't tell. You only show up on Sunday morning. You live thirty minutes away. I have no idea what your life looks like during the week. You've been church hopping for years. And you say you love Jesus, but which Jesus are you talking about? We have a hundred to choose from.

Societal Favor or Disfavor

A society's general posture toward Christianity also affects a church's ability to affirm and oversee professions of faith. Ironically, it can be easier in some ways to affirm and oversee Christians in a society that's outwardly opposed to the gospel. Think of first-century Palestine or Muslim nations today. In such locations there is a huge social disincentive to identify yourself with a church. As such, the people presenting themselves for baptism are less likely to be joining for the sake of social approval.

Now think of a society where cultural Christianity is prevalent. Baptism and membership are incentivized. Children will receive their parents' praise. Adults will receive an expanded prospective client list for their sales job or law firm.

Both of these categories of differences, I believe, will affect how much structure a church needs in order to fulfill its task with the tools Christ has given it. We're dealing in the realm of prudence here, which is never an exact science, but generally speaking I think we can say, the more social favor Christianity receives and the more complex a society is, the more structure a church may require.

In a complex society, membership classes, for instance, help you to know exactly which Jesus a church is talking about. The formal membership interview helps the church know which Jesus you are talking about. Both classes and interviews also help to set everyone's expectations.

In a complex society, furthermore, membership rolls help churches keep track of individuals spread out over large metropolitan areas. They help congregations and their leaders know who they are specifically responsible for.

But in a simpler society that disfavors Christianity, things like membership classes and membership rolls may be unnecessary and cumbersome. In fact, written rolls can be dangerous if they land in the wrong set of hands. That said, Jesus has still given such churches the same tools for the same task of being distinct. Let's see if I can illustrate this with our friends in central Asia.

THE BIBLICAL BASELINE

In Frank and Hanz's church, a person becomes a member upon baptism. Yet baptism always follows several weeks of being interviewed by the elders and the church. These interviews don't occur in church offices, which don't exist. They occur over walks and shared bowls of pilaf. Really, they feel more like conversations than interviews, but their purpose is the same: making sure a confessor understands the gospel and is repentant.

The individual will then be asked to make his or her profession in front of the whole congregation, at which time the members of the church ask questions. The elders lead the discussion, but they encourage everyone to participate since that helps to clarify everyone's understanding of the gospel.

The congregation never votes, but eventually a consensus will arise about whether the individual is a believer or needs a little longer to demonstrate the genuineness of his or her faith. In a Muslim community like this, it's expected that conversion changes people's lives, so the church looks for evidence of conversion. They don't expect everything to be cleaned up, but they do want to see the beginning of repentance, particularly the willingness to publicly identify before the church as a follower of Jesus.

As a final step, the church will give its affirmation through baptism, which officially welcomes the individual into the assembly. Of course, baptisms are logistically difficult to execute in this country. Sometimes they will be done in a pond or a river some distance from the city, although I had the privilege of witnessing one baptism in a wealthier individual's wading pool.

I believe this little congregation in central Asia provides us with a biblical baseline. It doesn't have all the structures of my own church, but I would argue that it fulfills the New Testament criteria of biblical church membership.

- It's plain to everyone who the members are, even though no formal membership roll exists. Everyone knows who has repented and believed and who hasn't, because everyone was present at the baptisms of everyone who joined after them. They also guard the communion table to help the line between church and world remain clear.
- The church carefully considers professions of faith to ensure faithfulness, even though there are no formal membership classes or one-off membership interviews. Besides, no cults or false churches have offered a different brand of Jesus or repentance—yet.
- Every member, including the elders, submits to the oversight of the entire church, even though there is no church

127

vote. Consensus is easy to recognize in a group of fifteen or twenty.

- The church practices discipline both to maintain church purity and to love the erring individual.

In all of this, Christ's name and fame are being protected and burnished.

A VERY DIFFERENT MODEL?

At first glance, the process of joining my church in Washington, DC, might look very different. You must begin by taking six membership classes, which cover our church's statement of faith, covenant, history, outreach work, and other elements of the congregation's life.

If you still want to join after that onslaught, you ask for a membership interview with an elder for sharing your testimony and explaining the gospel. One particular pastor is known for asking people to explain the good news "in sixty seconds or less"! At the conclusion of the interview, you will be asked to sign the church statement of faith and church covenant.

The elder, who has spent the entire interview filling out a membership form, photocopies the form for every elder, who is required to read it before the next elders' meeting. The elders consider your application together, vote on it using Robert's Rules of Order, and pass it along to the congregation at the next bimonthly members' meeting. After a two-minute introduction to you by an elder, your face hovering above on a PowerPoint slide, the congregation also votes on you, again aided by the punctilious Robert and his rules.

If you are voted in as a member, you will be placed on the membership roll and receive a membership packet, which contains a host of marginally useful items.

It all sounds pretty bureaucratic, doesn't it? And none of these details come from the Bible. I'm pretty sure Robert didn't travel with Paul and Barnabas. Maybe he was with Peter?

In fact, I'd say that a church in most secularized global cities today *simply cannot* do what the Bible commands churches to do in affirming and overseeing Christ's citizens without some set of structures *like* this. It doesn't have to be these structures. Maybe a church wants to require every prospective member to take a four-hour walk through the park with an elder and a couple other members in order to talk through all the matters that come up in a class and an interview. Maybe a church wants to require members to memorize names instead of writing them down.

The point is, some type of conversation needs to happen before a professing Christian and a church say "I do" in this covenant-like relationship called church membership. And a church needs to know who all its members are. After all, Jesus would have us be careful with *all* of his sheep.

In short, I believe the differences between the central Asian and American models are essentially cosmetic. Both churches are accomplishing the same objectives—the proclamation, display, and protection of the gospel through the lives of its formally affirmed members.

MEMBERSHIP MATTERS—CHRISTIAN LIFE MATTERS

In Frank and Hanz's church, contextual factors simplify the structures of membership. As one individual said to me, "Figuring out who is in and who is out is relatively easy." This became evident during recent police raids on the church, which made the members feel more conspicuous than ever.

The greater challenge for Frank and Hanz lies with teaching the members of the church about their new obligations to one another, as well as the purpose of church discipline. But for them, these lessons aren't so much membership matters as they are Christian life matters. The Christian life and church membership almost perfectly overlap for these blessed saints. They're the same thing.

So it should be with us.

CONCLUSION

How Church Membership Defines Love

Through the lives of its members, the local church defines love for the world.

This is good news because the world today is pretty confused about the definition of love. It thinks that love is like a glob of gelatin, something with no center, no parts, no hard edges. It thinks love is something that's free from all conditions, all expectations, all standards, all judgments. "♥ + ♥ = Marriage" says the bumper sticker. Even in Christian circles we pit love against law and truth, dividing the world into truth people and love people.

The only problem is, Jesus's love is not like that. Jesus's love begins with an act of mercy, and then it calls the recipients of mercy to the freedom of obedience.

- First, it's an act of mercy: "Greater love has no one than this: to lay down one's life for one's friends," said Jesus (John 15:13).
- Then, it's a call to obedience: "If you love me, keep my I commands" (John 14:15).

131

This is a combination that the world does not understand, but this is the love of God: love and holiness are not opposed to one another but partner together to lead people to God.

King Jesus then calls churches to put his same merciful and obedient love on display for the world: "A new command I give you: Love one another. As I have loved you, so you must love one another. By this everyone will know that you are my disciples, if you love one another" (John 13:34–35). So we lay down our lives for one another and then fight together for the freedom of obedience. When we do, we display Christ's love for the world and cause the nations to give praise.

FURTHER RESOURCES

1. My book *Church Discipline: How the Church Protects the Name of Jesus* (Crossway, 2012) is the companion book to this volume, which explains how to approach different scenarios that may call for discipline. It expands on the content of chapter 7.

2. A more in-depth biblical and theological treatment of the topics of this book can be found in my book *The Church and the Surprising Offense of God's Love: Reintroducing the Doctrines of Church Membership and Discipline* (Crossway, 2010).

3. Thabiti Anyabwile offers a wonderful meditation on how to pursue meaningful membership in his book *What Is a Healthy Church Member?* (Crossway, 2008).

4. If you haven't read Mark Dever's *What Is a Healthy Church?* (Crossway, 2007), you are missing a great introduction to what to look for in a healthy church.

5. A host of articles, book reviews, audio interviews, and short questions and answers on the topics of membership and discipline can be found at www.9Marks.org.

SPECIAL THANKS

Once again, a big thanks to Mark Dever, Matt Schmucker, and Ryan Townsend for supporting this work. Bobby Jamieson was the first to read it and offer good suggestions. Thanks, brothers. I love my job because of these men and the rest of the 9Marks staff.

Crossway is a wonderful publisher to work with. Thank you, Al Fisher and others.

Extra readers of the first manuscript, each of whom improved it, include Kendrick Kuo, Jeff Gearhart, Bill and Jane Englund, Robert Cline, and Jeramie Rinne. Thank you much, friends.

As always, my wonderful wife, Shannon, was a source of support and discussion about the book's contents. I'm so grateful for you, love.

Thank God with me, finally, for sending his Son to purchase a church that includes rebels like me.

NOTES

Chapter 1: We've Been Approaching It All Wrong
1. I would not say that these last two points are an absolute "requirement" either; I would say that baptism should *ordinarily* lead to membership, and that the Lord's Supper is *ordinarily* for church members.

2. Quoted in Janet Coleman, *Against the State: Studies in Sedition and Rebellion* (New York: Penguin, 1990), 37.

Chapter 3: What Is a Church? What Is a Church Member?
1. Edmund P. Clowney, *The Church,* Contours of Theology (Downers Grove, IL: InterVarsity, 1995), 40.

Chapter 4: What Are a Church and Its Members Like?
1. Walt Disney, *Pinocchio*, directed by Ben Sharpsteen (Burbank, CA: Walt Disney Studio, 1940), DVD.

2. *Back to the Future*, directed by Robert Zemeckis (Hollywood, CA: Universal Studios, 1985), DVD.

3. Dave Barry, *Dave Barry Slept Here: A Sort of History of the United States* (New York: Ballantine, 1997), 149.

4. T. S. Eliot, "The Waste Land" in *Collected Poems 1909–1962* (Boston: Faber & Faber, 1963), 63.

5. W. B. Yeats, "He Wishes for the Cloths of Heaven," *William Butler Yeats Selected Poems and Three Plays*, 3rd ed., edited by M. L. Rosenthal (New York: Collier, 1986), 27.

Chapter 7: What Happens When Members Don't Represent Jesus?
1. David Gergen, "It's Not Can We, but Will We?" *U.S. News & World Report*, September 24, 2001, 60.

SCRIPTURE INDEX

BE SURE TO CHECK OUT THESE OTHER
BOOKS BY **JONATHAN LEEMAN**

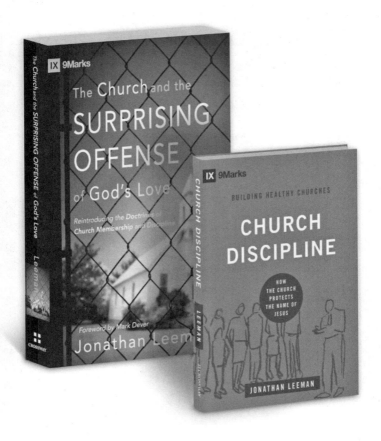

9MARKS: BUILDING HEALTHY CHURCHES SERIES

Based on Mark Dever's best-selling book *Nine Marks of a Healthy Church*, each book in this series helps readers grasp basic biblical commands regarding the local church.

TITLES INCLUDE:

Biblical Theology	Conversion	The Gospel
Church Discipline	Discipling	Missions
Church Elders	Evangelism	Sound Doctrine
Church Membership	Expositional Preaching	

For more information, visit crossway.org.
For translated versions of these and other 9Marks books, visit 9Marks.org/bookstore/translations.